JAMES

Guidelines for a Happy Christian Life

JOHN MACARTHUR

JAMES
MACARTHUR BIBLE STUDIES

Copyright © 2001, John F. MacArthur, Jr. Published by Word Publishing, P.O.
Box 141000, Nashville, TN 37214. All rights reserved. No portion of this book
may be reproduced, stored in a retrieval system, or transmitted in any form or
by any means—electronic, mechanical, photocopy, recording, or any other—
except for brief quotations in printed reviews, without the prior permission of
the publisher.

Scripture passages taken from:
The Holy Bible, *New King James Version*
Copyright © 1979, 1980, 1982 by Thomas Nelson. All rights reserved.

Cover Art by The Puckett Group.
Interior design and composition by Design Corps, Batavia, IL.

Produced with the assistance of the Livingstone Corporation. Project staff
include Dave Veerman, Christopher D. Hudson, and Amber Rae.

Project editor: Len Woods

ISBN 0-8499-5548-3

All rights reserved. *Printed in the United States of America.*

01 02 03 04 PHX 5 4 3

JAMES

Table of Contents

THE EPISTLE OF JAMES

Introduction

James, like all the general epistles except Hebrews, is named after its author (v. 1).

Author and Date

Of the four men named James in the New Testament, only two are candidates for authorship of this epistle. No one has seriously considered James the Less, the son of Alphaeus (Matt. 10:3; Acts 1:13), or James the father of Judas, not Iscariot (Luke 6:16; Acts 1:13). Some have suggested James the son of Zebedee and brother of John (Matt. 4:21), but he was martyred too early to have written it (Acts 12:2). That leaves only James, the oldest half brother of Christ (Mark 6:3) and brother of Jude (Matt. 13:55), who also wrote the epistle that bears his name (Jude 1). James had at first rejected Jesus as Messiah (John 7:5), but later believed (1 Cor. 15:7). He became the key leader in the Jerusalem church (see Acts 12:17; 15:13; 21:18; Gal. 2:12), being called one of the "pillars" of that church, along with Peter and John (Gal. 2:9). Also known as James the Just because of his devotion to righteousness, he was martyred ca. A.D. 62, according to the first-century Jewish historian Josephus. A comparison of James's vocabulary in his letter wrote recorded in Acts 15 with that in the epistle of James further corroborates his authorship.

James		Acts 15
1:1	"greetings"	15:23
1:16, 19; 2:5	"beloved"	15:25
1:21; 5:20	"your souls"	15:24
1:27	"visit"	15:14
2:10	"keep"	15:24
5:19, 20	"turn"	15:19

James wrote with the authority of one who had personally seen the resurrected Christ (1 Cor. 15:7), who was recognized as an associate of the apostles (Gal. 1:19), and who was the leader of the Jerusalem church.

James most likely wrote this epistle to believers scattered (1:1) as a result of the unrest recorded in Acts 12 (ca. A.D. 44). There is no mention of the Council of Jerusalem described in Acts 15 (ca. A.D. 49), which would be expected if that Council had already taken place. Therefore, James can be reliably dated ca. A.D. 44–49, making it the earliest written book of the New Testament canon.

Background and Setting

The recipients of this book were Jewish believers who had been dispersed (1:1), possibly as a result of Stephen's martyrdom (Acts 7, A.D. 31–34), but more likely due to the persecution under Herod Agrippa I (Acts 12, ca. A.D. 44). The author refers to his audience as "brethren" fifteen times (1:2, 16, 19; 2:1, 5, 14; 3:1, 10, 12; 4:11; 5:7, 9, 10, 12, 19); this was a common epithet among first-century Jews. Not surprisingly, then, James is Jewish in its content. For example, the Greek word translated "assembly" (2:2) is the word for "synagogue." Further, James contains more than forty allusions to the Old Testament (and more than twenty to the Sermon on the Mount, Matt. 5–7).

Historical and Theological Themes

James, with its devotion to direct, pungent statements on wise living, is reminiscent of the Book of Proverbs. It has a practical emphasis, stressing not theoretical knowledge but godly behavior. James wrote with a passionate desire for his readers to be uncompromisingly obedient to the Word of God. He uses at least thirty references to nature (e.g., "wave of the sea" [1:6]; "reptile" [3:7]; and "heaven gave rain" [5:18]), as befits one who spent a great deal of time outdoors. He complements Paul's emphasis on justification by faith with his own emphasis on spiritual fruitfulness demonstrating true faith.

Interpretive Challenges

At least two significant texts challenge the interpreter: (1) In 2:14–26, what is the relationship between faith and works? Does James's emphasis on works contradict Paul's focus on faith? (2) In 5:13–18, do the promises of healing refer to the spiritual or the physical realm? These difficult texts are treated in the notes.

Outline

There are a number of ways of outlining the book in order to grasp the arrangement of its content. One way is to arrange it around a series of tests by which the genuineness of a person's faith may be measured.

Introduction (1:1)

From Trouble to Triumph... and Back!

Opening Thought

1) Explain why the so-called health and wealth gospel is so popular in the North American church, especially when the New Testament paints a contrary picture of the life of faith—a life filled with hardship and trial.

_____

_____

_____

_____

2) Consider the church folk you know and have known. What have you observed as the most common "Christian" responses to trials and setbacks in their lives?

_____

_____

_____

_____

3) Describe a situation in which a believer you know has handled a difficult time with exceptional grace and humility. What made the difference? What was his or her "secret"?

_____

_____

_____

_____

Background of the Passage

James's major emphasis in this section of his epistle (and, really, in the entire letter) is this: If a person's faith is genuine, it will prove itself during times of trouble, whatever the nature or source of the trouble may be. For that reason, this epistle is valuable for unbelievers as well as believers. That is especially true for unbelievers who consider themselves to be Christians and need to recognize that a faith that is reliable only when things are going well is not saving faith and is worth nothing. It is, in fact, worth *less* than nothing, because it deceives those who trust in it. Not only will it fail them when they need help the most, but also it will lead them to think they are headed for heaven when, in reality, they are headed for hell.

The clear message of Scripture is that trials are a tool in the loving hands of the Lord. They test the strength of our faith; they humble us; they wean us from our dependence on earthly things; they call us to eternal and heavenly hope; they reveal what we really love; they teach us to value God's blessings; they develop enduring strength for greater usefulness; they help us better encourage others who are in times of trial.

Since trials are so productive, it is essential for us to respond rightly to them. James helps us greatly in this in 1:1–12 by giving five means for persevering through trials: a joyful attitude (v. 2), an understanding mind (v. 3), a submissive will (v. 4), a believing heart (vv. 5–8), and a humble spirit (vv. 9–11). He then tells us of the reward for perseverance (v. 12).

Bible Passage

Read James 1:1–12, noting the key words and definitions to the right of the passage.

James 1:1–12

¹ *James, a bondservant of God and of the Lord Jesus Christ,*
To the twelve tribes which are scattered abroad:
Greetings.
² *My brethren, count it all joy when you fall into various trials,*

James (v. 1)—the half brother of the Lord Jesus (see introduction: author and date)

twelve tribes (v. 1)—a common New Testament title for Jews. When the kingdom split after Solomon's reign, ten tribes constituted the northern kingdom, called Israel, and Benjamin and Judah

3 *knowing that the testing of your faith produces patience.*

4 *But let patience have its perfect work, that you may be perfect and complete, lacking nothing.*

5 *If any of you lacks wisdom, let him ask of God, who gives to all liberally and without reproach, and it will be given to him.*

6 *But let him ask in faith, with no doubting, for he who doubts is like a wave of the sea driven and tossed by the wind.*

7 *For let not that man suppose that he will receive anything from the Lord;*

8 *he is a double-minded man, unstable in all his ways.*

9 *Let the lowly brother glory in his exaltation,*

10 *but the rich in his humiliation, because as a flower of the field he will pass away.*

11 *For no sooner has the sun risen with a burning heat than it withers the grass; its flower falls, and its beautiful appearance perishes. So the rich man also will fade away in his pursuits.*

12 *Blessed is the man who endures temptation; for when he has been approved, he will receive the crown of life which the Lord has promised to those who love Him.*

combined to form the southern kingdom, called Judah. After the fall and deportation of the northern kingdom to Assyria (722 B.C.), some of the remnant of those in the ten northern tribes filtered down into Judah and came to Jerusalem to worship (2 Chr. 29, 30, 34), thus preserving all twelve tribes in Judah's land. Although tribal identity could not be established with certainty after the southern kingdom was led captive by Babylon (586 B.C.), the prophets foresaw a time when God would reconstitute the whole nation and delineate each person's tribal membership once again (see Is. 11:12–13; Jer. 3:18; 50:4; Rev. 7:5–8).

scattered abroad (v. 1)—The Greek word diaspora, which literally means "through a sowing" (see John 7:35), became a technical term referring to Jews living outside the land of Palestine (see 1 Pet. 1:1). Besides the expulsions from the land by the Assyrians (2 Kings 17; 1 Chr. 5) and Babylonians (2 Kings 24–25; 2 Chr. 36), many Jews were taken to Rome as slaves when the Romans conquered them ca. 63 B.C.; in addition, during the centuries leading up to Christ's first coming, thousands of Jews drifted out of Palestine and settled throughout the Mediterranean world. But James's primary audience was those who were scattered because of persecution.

brethren (v. 2)—believing Jews among those scattered

count it all joy (v. 2)—The Greek word for "count" may also be translated "consider" or "evaluate." The natural human response to trials is not to rejoice; therefore the believer must make a conscious commitment to face them with joy.

trials (v. 2)—This Greek word connotes trouble, or something that breaks the pattern of peace, comfort, joy, and happiness in someone's life. The verb form of this word means "to put someone or something to the test," with the purpose of discovering that person's nature or that thing's quality. God brings such tests to prove—and increase—the strength and quality of one's faith and to demonstrate its validity (vv. 2–12). Every trial becomes a test of faith designed to strengthen; if the believer fails the test by responding wrongly, that test then becomes a temptation, or a solicitation to evil.

testing (v. 3)—This means "proof" or "proving."

patience (v. 3)—better translated "endurance" or "perseverance"; through tests, a Christian will learn to withstand tenaciously the pressure of a trial until God removes it at His appointed time, at which point he will even cherish the benefit.

perfect (v. 4)—not a reference to sinless perfection (see 3:2), but rather to spiritual maturity; the testing of faith drives believers to deeper communion and greater trust in Christ—qualities that in turn produce a stable, godly, and righteous character

complete (v. 4)—from a compound Greek word that literally means "all the portions whole"

wisdom (v. 5)—James's Jewish audience recognized this as the understanding and practical skill that was necessary to live life to God's glory. It was not a wisdom of philosophical speculation, but the wisdom contained in the pure and peaceable absolutes of God's will revealed in His Word (see 3:13, 17) and lived out. Only such divine wisdom enables believers to be joyous and submissive in the trials of life.

ask of God (v. 5)—This command is a necessary part of the believer's prayer life. God intends that trials will drive believers to greater dependency on Him, by showing them their own inadequacy. As with all His riches (Eph. 1:7; 2:7; 3:8; Phil. 4:19), God has wisdom in abundance available for those who seek it.

ask in faith (v. 6)—Prayer must be offered with confident trust in a sovereign God.

with no doubting (v. 6)—This refers to having one's thinking divided within himself, not merely because of mental indecision but an inner moral conflict or distrust in God.

wave of the sea (v. 6)—The person who doubts God's ability or willingness to provide this wisdom is like the billowing, restless sea, moving back and forth with its endless tides, never able to settle.

double-minded man (v. 8)—a literal translation of the Greek expression that denotes having one's mind or soul divided between God and the world; this man is a hypocrite, who occasionally believes in God but fails to trust Him when trials come and thus receives nothing; the use of this expression in 4:8 makes it clear that it refers to an unbeliever

lowly brother ... the rich (vv. 9–10)—Trials make all believers equally dependent on God and bring them to the same level with each other by keeping them from becoming preoccupied with earthly things. Poor Christians and wealthy ones alike can rejoice that God is no respecter of persons and that they both have the privilege of being identified with Christ.

glory (v. 9)—This word refers to the boasting of a privilege or possession; it is the joy of legitimate pride. Although having nothing in this world, the poor believer can rejoice in his high spiritual standing before God by grace and the hope which that brings.

his humiliation (v. 10)—refers to the rich believer's being brought low by trials; such experiences help him rejoice and realize that genuine happiness and contentment depend on the true riches of God's grace, not earthly wealth

grass, flower (v. 11)—This pictures Palestine's flowers and flowering grasses, which colorfully flourish in February and dry up by May; and is a clear allusion to Isaiah 40:6–8, which speaks of the scorching sirocco wind that burns and destroys plants in its path. This picture from nature illustrates how divinely wrought death and judgment can quickly end the wealthy person's dependence on material possessions.

Blessed (v. 12)—Believers who successfully endure trials are truly happy (see 5:11).

endures (v. 12)—In this context, it also describes the passive, painful survival of a trial and focuses on the victorious outcome. Such a person never relinquishes his saving faith in God; thus this concept is closely related to the doctrine of eternal security and perseverance of the believer (see John 14:15, 23; 1 John 2:5, 6, 15, 19; 1 Pet. 1:6–8).

temptation (v. 12)—This is better translated "trials".

approved (v. 12)—literally "passed the test"; the believer has successfully and victoriously gone through his trials, indicating he is genuine because his faith has endured like Job's

crown of life (v. 12)—best translated "the crown which is life"; "crown" was the wreath put on the victor's head after ancient Greek athletic events; here, it denotes the believer's ultimate reward—eternal life—which God has promised to him and will grant in full at death or at Christ's coming

Understanding the Text

4) To whom did James address his letter?

_____

_____

_____

_____

_____

_____

_____

5) What does James say trials accomplish in the life of a believer?

_____

_____

_____

_____

_____

_____

_____

_____

(verses to consider: 2 Corinthians 12:7–10; 1 Peter 5:10)

6) How does James say that believers should respond to trials?

_____

_____

_____

_____

_____

_____

_____

(verses to consider: Proverbs 3:5–7; Acts 5:40–42; 1 Thessalonians 5:16–18; Hebrews 12:2–3)

7) What does it mean to be double-minded?

_____

_____

_____

_____

_____

_____

_____

8) When is boasting legitimate?

_____

_____

_____

_____

_____

_____

_____

(verses to consider: Jeremiah 9:23–24; 1 Corinthians 1:27–31)

Cross-Reference

Proverbs 3:1–26
 1 *My son, do not forget my law,*
   But let your heart keep my commands;
 2 *For length of days and long life*
   And peace they will add to you.

 3 *Let not mercy and truth forsake you;*
   Bind them around your neck,
   Write them on the tablet of your heart,
 4 *And so find favor and high esteem*
   In the sight of God and man.
 5 *Trust in the LORD with all your heart,*
   And lean not on your own understanding;
 6 *In all your ways acknowledge Him,*
   And He shall direct your paths.
 7 *Do not be wise in your own eyes;*
   Fear the LORD and depart from evil.
 8 *It will be health to your flesh,*
   And strength to your bones.
 9 *Honor the LORD with your possessions,*

And with the firstfruits of all your increase;
10 *So your barns will be filled with plenty,*
    And your vats will overflow with new wine.
11 *My son, do not despise the chastening of the Lord,*
    Nor detest His correction;
12 *For whom the* LORD *loves He corrects,*
    Just as a father the son in whom he delights.
13 *Happy is the man who finds wisdom,*
    And the man who gains understanding;
14 *For her proceeds are better than the profits of silver,*
    And her gain than fine gold.
15 *She is more precious than rubies,*
    And all the things you may desire cannot compare with her.
16 *Length of days is in her right hand,*
    In her left hand riches and honor.
17 *Her ways are ways of pleasantness,*
    And all her paths are peace.
18 *She is a tree of life to those who take hold of her,*
    And happy are all who retain her.
19 *The* LORD *by wisdom founded the earth;*
    By understanding He established the heavens;
20 *By His knowledge the depths were broken up,*
    And clouds drop down the dew.
21 *My son, let them not depart from your eyes—*
    Keep sound wisdom and discretion;
22 *So they will be life to your soul*
    And grace to your neck.
23 *Then you will walk safely in your way,*
    And your foot will not stumble.
24 *When you lie down, you will not be afraid;*
    Yes, you will lie down and your sleep will be sweet.
25 *Do not be afraid of sudden terror,*
    Nor of trouble from the wicked when it comes;
26 *For the* LORD *will be your confidence,*
    And will keep your foot from being caught.

Exploring the Meaning

9) What does this passage say about the importance of gaining wisdom?

_____

_____

_____

_____

_____

_____

_____

_____

10) Read Romans 11:33. What does this verse say about God's wisdom?

_____

_____

_____

_____

_____

_____

_____

11) Read Hebrews 11:1, 6. What do these verses say about the role of faith in our dealings with God?

_____

_____

_____

_____

_____

Summing Up

"To test the genuineness of a diamond, jewelers often place it in clear water, which causes a real diamond to sparkle with special brilliance. An imitation stone, on the other hand, will have almost no sparkle at all. When the two are placed side by side, even an untrained eye can easily tell the difference.

"In a similar way, even the world can often notice the marked differences between genuine Christians and those who merely profess faith in Christ. As with jewels, there is a noticeable difference in radiance, especially when people are undergoing difficult times. Many people have great confidence in their faith until it is severely tested by hardships and disappointments. How a person handles trouble will reveal whether his faith is living or dead, genuine or imitation, saving or non-saving."—*John MacArthur*

Reflecting on the Text

12) What trials are in your path right now? How can you take the truths of this lesson and glorify God in the midst of your difficulties?

_____

_____

_____

_____

_____

_____

_____

13) How would you define endurance in the Christian life? How would you rate yourself when it comes to clinging to God in faith through tough times?

How does one become more spiritually "tenacious"?

_____

_____

_____

_____

_____

_____

_____

14) According to James 1:12, why is it imperative that we persevere?

_____

_____

_____

_____

_____

_____

_____

(verses to consider: 2 Timothy 4:8; 1 Peter 5:4; Revelation 2:10)

Recording Your Thoughts

_____

_____

_____

_____

_____

_____

_____

_____

_____

_____

For further study, see the following passages:

Joshua 24:15	1 Kings 18:21	Proverbs 27:24
Ezekiel 37	Matthew 5:4,10, 11	Matthew 24:13
Romans 1:1	Galatians 1:19	Galatians 2:9
Philippians 3:1	1 Peter 1:1–2	1 John 4:19
Revelation 3:16		

The Fault for Temptation

James 1:13–18

Opening Thought

1) It has been observed that we currently live in a "culture of blame" and that we no longer have a sense of shame about anything. Everyone has a rationalization, explanation, or excuse for why they do evil. Do you agree this is a growing trend? Why or why not? What do you think is the cause of this?

_____

_____

_____

_____

2) What are some of the more ridiculous "excuses" you have heard for people doing what is clearly wrong?

_____

_____

_____

_____

3) What makes it so hard for people caught red-handed in wrongdoing to own up to their guilt?

_____

_____

_____

_____

Background of the Passage

Just as it is common for man to be tempted (1 Cor. 10:13), it is also common for him to blame someone or something else, not only for his being tempted but also for his succumbing to it. From the beginning, one of the chief characteristics of sin has been the propensity to pass off blame, and every parent knows that children are born with that very evident propensity.

When God confronted Adam with his sin in the Garden of Eden, Adam's reply was, "The woman whom You gave to be with me, she gave me from the tree, and I ate" (Gen. 3:12). When the Lord then asked Eve, "What is this you have done?" she replied, "The serpent deceived me, and I ate" (v. 13). Eve blamed Satan; much worse, Adam blamed God.

In his fierce opposition to the ungodly rationalization of blaming God for sending enticement to evil, James gives four strong proofs that He is not responsible for our temptations and even less responsible, if that were possible, for our succumbing to them in sin. He does so by explaining the nature of evil (1:13b), the nature of man (v. 14), the nature of lust (vv. 15–16), and the nature of God (v. 17). In verse 18, he gives a fifth proof, the nature of regeneration.

Bible Passage

Read James 1:13–18, noting the key words and definitions to the right of the passage.

James 1:13–18

13 *Let no one say when he is tempted, "I am tempted by God"; for God cannot be tempted by evil, nor does He Himself tempt anyone.*

14 *But each one is tempted when he is drawn away by his own desires and enticed.*

15 *Then, when desire has conceived, it gives birth to sin; and sin, when it is full-grown, brings forth death.*

16 *Do not be deceived, my beloved brethren.*

17 *Every good gift and every perfect gift is from*

tempted (v. 13)—The same Greek word translated "trials" (vv. 2–12) is also translated "temptation" here. James's point is that every difficult circumstance that enters a believer's life can either strengthen him, if he obeys God and remains confident in His care, or become a solicitation to evil, if he chooses instead to doubt God and disobey His Word.

God cannot be tempted (v. 13)—God by His holy nature has no capacity for evil or vulnerability to it.

above, and comes down from the Father of lights, with whom there is no variation or shadow of turning.

18 *Of His own will He brought us forth by the word of truth, that we might be a kind of firstfruits of His creatures.*

nor does He Himself tempt anyone (v. 13)—God purposes trials to occur and in them He allows temptation to happen, but He has promised not to allow more than believers can endure and never without a way to escape; they choose whether to take the escape God provides or to give in.

drawn away (v. 14)—This Greek word was used to describe wild game being lured into traps. Just as animals can be drawn to their deaths by attractive baits, temptation promises people something good, which is actually harmful.

his own desires (v. 14)—This refers to lust, the strong desire of the human soul to enjoy or acquire something to fulfill the flesh. Man's fallen nature has the propensity to strongly desire whatever sin will satisfy it; "his own" describes the individual nature of lust—it is different for each person as a result of inherited tendencies, environment, upbringing, and personal choices. The Greek grammar also indicates that these "desires" are the direct agent or cause of one's sinning.

enticed (v. 14)—a fishing term that means "to capture" or "to catch with bait"; it is a parallel to "drawn away"

has conceived…gives birth…brings forth (v. 15)—Sin is not merely a spontaneous act, but the result of a process. The Greek words for "has conceived" and "brings forth" liken the process to physical conception and birth; thus James personifies temptation and shows that it can follow a similar sequence and produce sin with all its deadly results. While sin does not result in spiritual death for the believer, it can lead to physical death.

Do not be deceived (v. 16)—The Greek expression refers to erring, going astray, or wandering. Christians are not to make the mistake of blaming God rather than themselves for their sin.

Every good ... perfect gift is from above (v. 17)—Two different Greek words for "gift" emphasize the perfection and inclusiveness of God's graciousness; the first denotes the act of giving, and the second is the object given. Everything related to divine giving is adequate, complete, and beneficial.

Father of lights (v. 17)—an ancient Jewish expression for God as the Creator, with "lights" referring to the sun, moon, and stars

no variation or shadow of turning (v. 17)—From man's perspective, the celestial bodies have different phases of movement and rotation, change from day to night, and vary in intensity and shadow; but God does not follow that pattern—He is changeless.

Of His own will (v. 18)—This phrase translates a Greek word that makes the point that regeneration is not just a wish, but an active expression of God's will, which He always has the power to accomplish. This phrase occurs at the beginning of the Greek sentence, which means James intends to emphasize that the sovereign will of God is the source of this new life.

He brought us forth (v. 18)—the divine act of regeneration, or the new birth

word of truth (v. 18)—Scripture, or the Word of God; He regenerates sinners through the power of that Word.

firstfruits (v. 18)—originally an Old Testament expression referring to the first and best harvest crops, which God expected as an offering (see Ex. 23:19; Deut. 26:1–19); giving God that initial crop was an act of faith that He would fulfill His promise of a full harvest to come; in the same way, Christians are the first evidence of God's new creation that is to come and enjoy presently in their new life a foretaste of future glory

Understanding the Text

4) What does James say about God and temptation?

_____

_____

_____

_____

_____

(verses to consider: Leviticus 19:2; Isaiah 6:3; Habakkuk 1:13; 1 Peter 1:16)

5) How does James describe the progression from temptation to sin?

_____

_____

_____

_____

_____

_____

6) What does James mean when he says that in God there is "no variation or shadow of turning" (v. 17)?

_____

_____

_____

_____

_____

(verses to consider: Malachi 3:6; Hebrews 13:8)

Cross-Reference

Romans 7:8–25

⁸ But sin, taking opportunity by the commandment, produced in me all manner of evil desire. For apart from the law sin was dead.

⁹ I was alive once without the law, but when the commandment came, sin revived and I died.

¹⁰ And the commandment, which was to bring life, I found to bring death.

¹¹ For sin, taking occasion by the commandment, deceived me, and by it killed me.

¹² Therefore the law is holy, and the commandment holy and just and good.

¹³ Has then what is good become death to me? Certainly not! But sin, that it might appear sin, was producing death in me through what is good, so that sin through the commandment might become exceedingly sinful.

¹⁴ For we know that the law is spiritual, but I am carnal, sold under sin.

¹⁵ For what I am doing, I do not understand. For what I will to do, that I do not practice; but what I hate, that I do.

¹⁶ If, then, I do what I will not to do, I agree with the law that it is good.

¹⁷ *But now, it is no longer I who do it, but sin that dwells in me.*

¹⁸ *For I know that in me (that is, in my flesh) nothing good dwells; for to will is present with me, but how to perform what is good I do not find.*

¹⁹ *For the good that I will to do, I do not do; but the evil I will not to do, that I practice.*

²⁰ *Now if I do what I will not to do, it is no longer I who do it, but sin that dwells in me.*

²¹ *I find then a law, that evil is present with me, the one who wills to do good.*

²² *For I delight in the law of God according to the inward man.*

²³ *But I see another law in my members, warring against the law of my mind, and bringing me into captivity to the law of sin which is in my members.*

²⁴ *O wretched man that I am! Who will deliver me from this body of death?*

²⁵ *I thank God—through Jesus Christ our Lord! So then, with the mind I myself serve the law of God, but with the flesh the law of sin.*

Exploring the Meaning

7) What does this passage from Romans say about the internal struggle Christians have between enticement to evil and desire for God-honoring righteous living?

_____

_____

_____

_____

8) Read John 3:3–8. What has God done in the life of each believer that, in effect, gives them no excuse for sin?

_____

_____

_____

_____

(verses to consider: Ezekiel 36:25–27; John 1:12–13; Ephesians 2:5–6)

9) Read Colossians 1:5. What part does the Word of God play in our victory over sin's penalty and power?

_____

_____

_____

_____

(verses to consider: Psalm 119:11; 1 Thessalonians 2:13; 2 Timothy 3:15–17; 1 Peter 1:23–25)

Summing Up . . .

"The new birth results from God's sovereignly coming down to a sinner and by His grace cleansing him, planting His Spirit within him, and giving him a completely new spiritual nature. He then has 'put on the new self, which in the likeness of God has been created in righteousness and holiness of the truth' (Ephesians 4:24).

"After Augustine was converted, a woman he had formerly lived with called to him as he walked down the street, but he did not answer. She persisted and finally ran up to him and said, 'Augustine, it is I.' To which he replied, 'I know, but it is no longer I.'"—*John MacArthur*

Reflecting on the Text

10) How much are you tempted to blame other people or circumstances for your own sin? What have you learned in this lesson about that tendency?

_____

_____

_____

_____

_____

11) How would it change your life today (specifically and practically) if you could remember in each moment that the old you is dead and that God has given you a new nature (2 Corinthians 5:17) that loves God and hates sin?

_____

_____

_____

_____

_____

12) Pick one verse from this lesson that has proven especially meaningful to you. Write it out in the space below. Commit it to memory.

_____

_____

_____

_____

_____

Recording Your Thoughts

_____

_____

_____

_____

_____

For further study, see the following passages:

Genesis 1:14–19	Leviticus 23:9–14	Proverbs 3:9–10
Matthew 15:18–20	John 17:17	Romans 8:19–23
1 Corinthians 11:30	2 Corinthians 6:7	Ephesians 5:26
Titus 3:5	James 4:7	2 Peter 2:14, 18
2 Peter 3:10–13	1 John 5:16	

Belief that Behaves

Opening Thought

1) Rank the following behaviors in order of how reliable you think they are in pointing out true saving faith (e.g. 1 = definitely a mark of a genuine believer; 10 = not necessarily indicative of anything):

_____ wears Christian T-shirts and jewelry

_____ has Christian bumper stickers on car (and drives the speed limit!)

_____ gives regularly and sacrificially to the church

_____ participates in regular missions and outreach efforts

_____ sings in the choir (sometimes even solos)

_____ studies God's Word regularly and seeks to live it

_____ attends church faithfully

_____ has healthy, loving relationships with friends, family, co-workers, church members, and neighbors

_____ prays fervently for the lost

_____ owns all of Dr. MacArthur's writings and listens to all his sermons on tape

2) Why did you rank the items as you did? What criteria did you use?

_____

_____

_____

3) What are the best indicators of true, saving faith?

_____

_____

_____

Background of the Passage

In the passage before us, James presents a third test of a true believer. The first was his response to trials (1:1–12). The second was his response to temptation (1:13–18). The third is his response to the truth revealed in the Word of God (1:19–27).

When the true disciple hears God's Word, there is an affection for its truth and a desire in his heart to obey it. One of the most reliable evidences of genuine salvation is that hunger for the Word of God (see Psalm 42:1). In 1:19–27, James focuses on two major truths relating to that evidence. First, saving faith is marked by a proper reception of Scripture as the Word of God (vv. 19–21). Second, it is marked by a proper reaction to the Word, reflected in an obedient life (vv. 22–27).

Just as a newborn baby does not have to be taught to hunger for its mother's milk, the newborn child of God does not have to be taught to hunger for God's Word, his spiritual food and drink. That is the natural impulse of his new spiritual life, of his new creation. To use another metaphor, his spiritual dial is tuned to the frequency of Scripture.

Bible Passage

Read James 1:19–27, noting the key words and definitions to the right of the passage.

James 1:19–27

19 *So then, my beloved brethren, let every man be swift to hear, slow to speak, slow to wrath;*

20 *for the wrath of man does not produce the righteousness of God.*

21 *Therefore lay aside all filthiness and overflow of wickedness, and receive with meekness the implanted word, which is able to save your souls.*

22 *But be doers of the word, and not hearers only, deceiving yourselves.*

23 *For if anyone is a hearer of the word and not a doer, he is like a man observing his natural face in a mirror;*

swift to hear, slow to speak (v. 19)—Believers are to respond positively to Scripture and eagerly pursue every opportunity to know God's Word and will better. At the same time, they should be cautious about becoming a preacher or teacher themselves.

wrath (v. 20)—from the Greek word that describes a deep, internal resentment and rejection, in this context, of God's Word

lay aside (v. 21)—literally "having put off," as one would do with dirty clothes; the tense of this

²⁴ *for he observes himself, goes away, and immediately forgets what kind of man he was.*

²⁵ *But he who looks into the perfect law of liberty and continues in it, and is not a forgetful hearer but a doer of the work, this one will be blessed in what he does.*

²⁶ *If anyone among you thinks he is religious, and does not bridle his tongue but deceives his own heart, this one's religion is useless.*

²⁷ *Pure and undefiled religion before God and the Father is this: to visit orphans and widows in their trouble, and to keep oneself unspotted from the world.*

Greek verb stresses the importance of putting off sin prior to receiving God's Word

filthiness … wickedness (v. 21)—The first term was used of moral vice as well as dirty garments; sometimes it was even used of ear wax—here, of sin that would impede the believer's spiritual hearing. "Wickedness" refers to evil desire or intent.

be doers (v. 22)—The fact that James calls professing believers "doers," rather than simply speaking of their actions, emphasizes that their entire personality should be characterized in that way.

deceiving (v. 22)—literally "reasoning beside or alongside" (as in "beside oneself"); this word was used in mathematics to refer to a miscalculation; professing Christians who are content with only hearing the Word have made a serious spiritual miscalculation

observing (v. 23)— look carefully and cautiously, as opposed to taking a casual glance

mirror (v. 23)—First-century mirrors were not glass but metallic, made of bronze, silver—or for the wealthy—gold. The metals were beaten flat and polished to a high gloss, and the image they reflected was adequate but not perfect.

forgets what kind of man he was (v. 24)—Unless professing Christians act promptly after they hear the Word, they will forget the changes and improvements that their reflection showed them they need to make.

perfect law (v. 25)—In both the Old and New Testaments, God's revealed, inerrant, sufficient, and comprehensive Word is called "law." The presence of His grace does not mean there is no moral law or code of conduct for believers to obey; rather, believers are enabled by the Spirit to keep this law.

liberty (v. 25)—genuine freedom from sin; as the Holy Spirit applies the principles of Scripture to believers' hearts, they are freed from sin's bondage and enabled to obey God

religious (v. 26)—This refers to ceremonial public worship. James chose this term, instead of one referring to internal godliness, to emphasize the external trappings, rituals, routines, and forms that were not followed sincerely.

bridle his tongue (v. 26)—"Bridle" means "control," or as another translation renders it, "keep a tight rein"; purity of heart is often revealed by controlled and proper speech.

Pure and undefiled religion (v. 27)—James picks two synonymous adjectives to define the most spotless kind of religious faith—that which is measured by compassionate love.

orphans and widows (v. 27)—Those without parents or husbands were and are an especially needy segment of the church. Since they are usually unable to reciprocate in any way, caring for them clearly demonstrates true, sacrificial Christian love.

world (v. 27)—the evil world system

Understanding the Text

4) According to James, what is the right response of a child of God to the Word of God?

_____

_____

_____

_____

_____

(verses to consider: Psalm 119:1, 10, 11, 14; 2 Timothy 2:15; 1 John 2:24; 3:10)

5) What does James 1:21 say we must do before we can properly receive God's Word? How exactly do we do this?

_____

_____

_____

_____

_____

_____

_____

(verses to consider: Romans 13:12–14; Ephesians 4:22–24; Colossians 3:8; Hebrews 12:1; 1 Peter 2:1–2)

6) What examples does James give as behavior indicative of true faith? Why do you think he chooses these particular actions?

_____

_____

_____

_____

_____

_____

(verses to consider: Exodus 22:22–23; Deuteronomy 14:28–29; Psalm 68:5; Jeremiah 7:6–7; John 13:35; Acts 6:1–6; 1 Timothy 5:3)

Cross-Reference

Read John 14:21–24:

²¹ *"He who has My commandments and keeps them, it is he who loves Me. And he who loves Me will be loved by My Father, and I will love him and manifest Myself to him."*

²² *Judas (not Iscariot) said to Him, "Lord, how is it that You will manifest Yourself to us, and not to the world?"*

²³ *Jesus answered and said to him, "If anyone loves Me, he will keep My word; and My Father will love him, and We will come to him and make Our home with him.*

²⁴ *"He who does not love Me does not keep My words; and the word which you hear is not Mine but the Father's who sent Me."*

Exploring the Meaning

7) How does this teaching of Jesus add to your understanding of the relationship between true saving faith and obedience to the Word? What does obedience demonstrate?

_____

_____

_____

_____

8) Read Romans 8:4. What resource does God give His children to ensure that they are able to live obediently?

_____

_____

_____

_____

(verses to consider: John 8:31–36; 16:7–15; Galatians 5:16–26)

9) Read James 4:4. What is the "world" and how does it seek to discourage us from obeying God's Word?

_____

_____

_____

_____

(verses to consider: Matthew 10:37–39; John 15:18–20; Philippians 3:20; 1 John 2:15–17)

Summing Up . . .

"As important as the proper reception of the Word of God is, without obedience to its truths it is not only without benefit but becomes a further judgment against its readers. It is essential to hear the Word with an attitude of submission, but even that is not enough. Obedience to the Word is the most basic spiritual requirement and is the common denominator for all true believers. The bottom line of true spiritual life is not a momentary feeling of compliance or commitment but long-term obedience to Scripture."
—*John MacArthur*

Reflecting on the Text

10) Why is humility necessary in hearing and obeying God's Word (James 1:21)? When do you find it most difficult to approach Scripture with a humble heart and a teachable spirit? Why do you think?

_____

_____

_____

_____

_____

11) Are you aware of any specific situations in your life in which you are not doing what you know God's Word calls you to do? Why the reluctance on your part to obey? What are the potential consequences of your disobedience? How could Christian friends help you in this struggle?

_____

_____

_____

_____

12) Many Christians possess a lot of biblical information (in fact, they read

books and go to conferences to acquire more and more head knowledge!). Unfortunately, many of these same folks do not allow this eternal truth to bring about God's desired transformation in their lives.

What action can you take today to keep you from this common (but sinful) tendency?

_____

_____

_____

_____

_____

Recording Your Thoughts

_____

_____

_____

_____

_____

_____

_____

_____

_____

_____

For further study, see the following passages:

Psalm 19:7	Ezekiel 3:17	Ezekiel 33:6–7
Matthew 7:21–27	Matthew 12:36–37	Acts 26:5
1 Corinthians 13:12	Galatians 4:16	1 Timothy 3:6
1 John 1:9		

Favoritism in the Church?

Opening Thought

1) It has been said that the most segregated time of the week in this culture is the Sunday morning worship hour. Do you agree? If this is true, why do you think it is so?

_____

_____

_____

_____

_____

_____

_____

2) Which of the following differences are the hardest to overcome in the church and why: financial, racial, cultural, generational, gender, theological, social, or other?

_____

_____

_____

_____

_____

_____

_____

Background of the Passage

An attribute of God that is not thought or spoken of often is His impartiality. Yet this is a serious and recurring theme throughout Scripture. God is absolutely impartial in His dealings with people. And in that way, as with His other attributes, He is unlike us. Human beings, even Christians, are not naturally inclined to be impartial. We tend to put people in pigeonholes, in predetermined, stratified categories, ranking them by their looks, their clothes, their race or ethnicity, their social status, their personality, their intelligence, their wealth and power, by the kind of car they drive, and by the type of house and neighborhood they live in. But all of those things are non-issues with God, of no significance or meaning to Him whatsoever.

The Epistle of James is very practical, dealing much more with day-to-day issues than with theology and doctrine in the usual sense. In this lesson's passage, he stresses that our partiality or lack of it is another test of living faith. The first test relates to how we respond to trials (1:1–12); the second to how we respond to temptation (1:13–18); the third to how we react to the Word of God (1:19–27); and the fourth to partiality, or favoritism (2:1–13). In the fourth one, he focuses mostly on partiality in regard to social and economic status, doubtless because those were special problems in the early church and were obviously problems with some of the Jewish believers "who [were] dispersed abroad" (1:1).

In 2:1–13, James presents five features of genuine, Godlike impartiality: the principle (v. 1), the example (vv. 2–4), the inconsistency (vv. 5–7), the violation (vv. 8–11), and the appeal (vv. 12–13).

Bible Passage

Read James 2:1–13, noting the key words and definitions to the right of the passage.

James 2:1–13

¹ *My brethren, do not hold the faith of our Lord Jesus Christ, the Lord of glory, with partiality.*
² *For if there should come into your assembly a*

the faith (v. 1—This refers not to the act of believing, but to the entire Christian faith (see Jude 3), which has as its central focus Jesus Christ.

man with gold rings, in fine apparel, and there should also come in a poor man in filthy clothes,

3 and you pay attention to the one wearing the fine clothes and say to him, "You sit here in a good place," and say to the poor man, "You stand there," or, "Sit here at my footstool,"

4 have you not shown partiality among yourselves, and become judges with evil thoughts?

5 Listen, my beloved brethren: Has God not chosen the poor of this world to be rich in faith and heirs of the kingdom which He promised to those who love Him?

6 But you have dishonored the poor man. Do not the rich oppress you and drag you into the courts?

7 Do they not blaspheme that noble name by which you are called?

8 If you really fulfill the royal law according to the Scripture, "You shall love your neighbor as yourself," you do well;

9 but if you show partiality, you commit sin, and are convicted by the law as transgressors.

10 For whoever shall keep the whole law, and yet stumble in one point, he is guilty of all.

11 For He who said, "Do not commit adultery," also said, "Do not murder." Now if you do not commit adultery, but you do murder, you have become a transgressor of the law.

12 So speak and so do as those who will be judged by the law of liberty.

13 For judgment is without mercy to the one who has shown no mercy. Mercy triumphs over judgment.

the Lord of glory (v. 1)—Christ is the One who reveals the glory of God. In His incarnation, He showed only impartiality (see Matt. 22:16)—for example, consider the variety of people included in His genealogy, His choice of the humble village of Nazareth as His residence for thirty years, and His willingness to minister in Galilee and Samaria, both regions held in contempt by Israel's leaders.

partiality (v. 1)— This word originally referred to raising someone's face or elevating the person, but it came to refer to exalting someone strictly on a superficial, external basis, such as appearance, race, wealth, rank, or social status.

assembly (v. 2)—literally "a gathering together" or "synagogue"; since James was writing early in the church's history to Jewish believers (1:1), he used both this general word and the normal Greek word for "church" (5:14) to describe the church's corporate meetings during that period of transition

gold rings (v. 2)—While Jews commonly wore rings, few could afford gold ones; however, there are some reports that in the ancient world the most ostentatious people wore rings on every finger but the middle one to show off their economic status (some ancient sources indicate that there were even ring rental businesses).

fine apparel (v. 2)—This word refers to bright, shining garments and is used of the gorgeous garment Herod's soldiers put on Jesus to mock Him, and of the apparel of an angel. It can also refer to bright, flashy color and to brilliant, glittering, sparkling ornamentation. James is not condemning this unbeliever for his distracting dress, but rather the church's flattering reaction to it.

a poor man (v. 2)—Although there were people of means in the early church (1 Tim. 6:17–19), it consisted mostly of common, poor people (see James 5; Acts 2:45). Throughout Scripture, the poor are objects of God's special concern (1:27).

sit … in a good place (v. 3)–a more comfortable, prominent place of honor. The synagogues and assembly halls of the first century sometimes had benches around the outside wall and a couple of benches in front; but most of the congregation either sat cross-legged on the floor or stood. There were a limited number of good seats; and they were the ones the Pharisees always wanted (Mark 12:38–39).

shown partiality (v. 4)—the true nature of the sin in this passage, not the lavish apparel or rings of the rich man or that he was given a good seat

judges with evil thoughts (v. 4)—This is better translated "judges with vicious intentions." James feared that his readers would behave just like the sinful world by catering to the rich and prominent while shunning the poor and common.

the kingdom (v. 5)—Here James intends the kingdom in its present sense of the sphere of salvation—those over whom Christ rules—as well as its future millennial and eternal glory.

oppress (v. 6)—literally "to tyrannize"

drag you into the courts (v. 6)—a reference to civil court

blaspheme that noble name (v. 7)—probably a reference to religious courts; wealthy Jewish opponents of Christ were harassing these poor Christians

royal law (v. 8)—This is better translated "sovereign law"; the idea is that this law is supreme or binding.

love your neighbor as yourself (v. 8)—This sovereign law, when combined with the command to love God, summarizes all the Law and the Prophets. James is not advocating some kind of emotional affection for one's self, for self-love is clearly a sin; rather, the command is to pursue meeting the physical health and spiritual well-being of one's neighbors (all within the sphere of our influence; Luke 10:30–37) with the same intensity and concern as one does naturally for one's self (see Phil. 2:3–4).

if (v. 9)—better translated as "since," the Greek construction of this conditional statement indicates that this practice was in fact happening among James's readers.

show partiality (v. 9)—The form of this Greek verb indicates that their behavior was not an occasional slip but a continual practice.

convicted by the law (v. 9)—specifically by the commands in Deuteronomy 1:17 and 16:19.

transgressors (v. 9)—This refers to one who goes beyond the law of God. Respect of persons makes one a violator of God's law.

whole law … one point (v. 10)—The law of God is not a series of detached injunctions but a basic unity that requires perfect love of Him and our neighbors. Although all sins are not equally damaging or heinous, they all shatter that unity and render men transgressors, much like hitting a window with a hammer at only one point will shatter and destroy the whole window.

guilty of all (v. 10)—not in the sense of having violated every command, but in the sense of having violated the law's unity; one transgression makes fulfilling the law's most basic commands—to love God perfectly and to love one's neighbor as oneself—impossible

the one who has shown no mercy (v. 13)—The person who shows no mercy and compassion for people in need demonstrates that he has never responded to the great mercy of God, and as an unredeemed person will receive only strict, unrelieved judgment in eternal hell (see Matt. 5:7).

Mercy triumphs over judgment (v. 13)—The person whose life is characterized by mercy is ready for the day of judgment and he will escape all the charges that strict justice might bring against him because by showing mercy to others he gives proof of having received God's mercy.

Understanding the Text

3) Why does James say that partiality is incompatible with faith?

_____

_____

_____

_____

_____

_____

_____

(verses to consider: Leviticus 19:15; Deuteronomy 10:17; 15:7–10; 2 Chronicles 19:7; Job 34:19; Proverbs 24:23; 28:21; Acts 10:34–35; Romans 2:11; Ephesians 6:9; 1 Peter 1:17)

4) Was the early church primarily composed of rich people or poor? What do you base your answer on?

_____

_____

_____

_____

_____

_____

5) What reaction did the poor often get when they visited a Christian assembly? What did James remind his readers about the poor?

_____

_____

_____

_____

_____

_____

_____

(verses to consider: Leviticus 25:35–37; Psalm 41:1; 72:4, 12; 113:7; Proverbs 17:5; 21:13; 28:27; 29:7; 31:9; Isaiah 3:14–15; 10:1–2; 25:4; Galatians 2:10)

Cross-Reference

Read Matthew 22:34–40.

34 *But when the Pharisees heard that He had silenced the Sadducees, they gathered together.*

35 *Then one of them, a lawyer, asked Him a question, testing Him, and saying,*

36 *"Teacher, which is the great commandment in the law?"*

37 *Jesus said to him, " 'You shall love the LORD your God with all your heart, with all your soul, and with all your mind.'*

38 *"This is the first and great commandment.*

39 *"And the second is like it: 'You shall love your neighbor as yourself.'*

40 *"On these two commandments hang all the Law and the Prophets."*

Exploring the Meaning

6) How do these verses, if obeyed, eliminate the sin of partiality among people of faith?

_____

_____

_____

_____

_____

_____

_____

(verses to consider: Deuteronomy 6:4–5; Romans 13:8–10)

7) Read 2 Timothy 3:2. How does this verse shatter the common myth that the command "love your neighbor as yourself" is actually a call for people to love themselves?

_____

_____

_____

_____

_____

_____

_____

8) Read Philippians 2:3–4. What does this passage (and its context) say about our attitudes and dealing with others?

_____

_____

_____

_____

_____

_____

_____

Summing Up . . .

"There will be no poor in heaven in any sense, no second-class citizens. Everyone will be rich in the things that matter eternally. Every believer will receive the same eternal life, the same heavenly citizenship in the kingdom of God, and the same perfect righteousness of Christ imputed to them by the Father. Every one of His children will live in His house and bask alike in His presence and love (John 14:1–3)."—*John MacArthur*

Reflecting on the Text

9) How specifically can you avoid showing partiality this week in your home? In the workplace? In the neighborhood? At church?

_____

_____

_____

_____

_____

_____

_____

10) Numerous passages in Scripture call on believers to show compassion to the poor. What are two or three concrete ways you can obey this command this week?

_____

_____

_____

_____

_____

_____

_____

_____

11) What are some ways of labeling others that you need to refrain from using immediately?

_____

_____

_____

_____

_____

_____

_____

Recording Your Thoughts

_____

_____

_____

_____

_____

_____

_____

For further study, see the following passages:

Matthew 3:2	Luke 15:22	Luke 23:11
John 1:14	John 16:2–4	Acts 10:30
Romans 2:6–16	Romans 8:29	1 Corinthians 1:26–29
2 Corinthians 4:4–6	Hebrews 1:1–3	Jude 3
Revelation 1:6		

Dead Faith!

James 2:14–20

Opening Thought

1) In a Sunday school class, the subject is salvation (and the life change that should accompany genuine conversion and regeneration). A class member brings up the real-life example of a professing Christian who has been struggling valiantly to come out of the homosexual lifestyle. After regular counseling, visits to "noted prayer warriors and specialists in deliverance," intense programs of personal Bible study and Scripture memory, and long-term, serious involvement in a church discipleship program, this individual has slipped back into his old way of living. He admits he's miserable, but he feels helpless to change.

Some argue that this decision calls into question the genuineness of this man's salvation experience. Others disagree, asking, "How is his struggle any different than the lifelong gossip (or glutton or angry person) who doesn't even make a serious effort to change (but whose faith is never questioned)?"

Who's right in this debate? How do we answer this ticklish, tough dilemma? Is this man's faith genuine and living (though obviously immature!) or is it spurious and dead?

_____

_____

_____

_____

_____

_____

_____

Background of the Passage

In this lesson, James continues his series of tests by which his readers can evaluate whether their faith is living or dead. This passage contains the composite test—the one test that pulls the others together: the test of works, or righteous behavior that obeys God's Word and manifests a godly nature (see 1:22–25).

James's point is not that a person is saved by works (he has already strongly and clearly asserted in 1:17–18 that salvation is a gracious gift from God), but that there is a kind of apparent faith that is dead and does not save (vv. 14, 17, 20, 24, 26). It is possible James was writing to Jews (see 1:1) who had jettisoned the works righteousness of Judaism but, instead, had embraced the mistaken notion that since righteous works and obedience to God's law were not efficacious for salvation, they were not necessary at all. Thus they reduced faith to a mere mental assent to the facts about Christ.

The truth that James emphasizes in this text and that the Word of God teaches throughout is that what we do reveals who we are. James is not speaking simply of beliefs and intentions in general but of the foundational belief of saving faith. The genuineness of a profession of Jesus Christ as Savior and Lord is evidenced more by what a person does than by what he claims. A person who professes Christ but who does not live a Christ-honoring, Christ-obeying life is a fraud.

Bible Passage

Read James 2:14–20, noting the key words and definitions to the right of the passage.

James 2:14–20

14 *What does it profit, my brethren, if someone says he has faith but does not have works? Can faith save him?*

15 *If a brother or sister is naked and destitute of daily food,*

16 *and one of you says to them, "Depart in peace, be warmed and filled," but you do not give them*

if someone says (v. 14)—This important phrase governs the interpretation of the entire passage. James does not say that this person actually has faith, but that he claims to have it.

faith (v. 14)—This is best understood in a broad sense, speaking of any degree of acceptance of the truths of the gospel.

the things which are needed for the body, what does it profit?

17 Thus also faith by itself, if it does not have works, is dead.

18 But someone will say, "You have faith, and I have works." Show me your faith without your works, and I will show you my faith by my works.

19 You believe that there is one God. You do well. Even the demons believe—and tremble!

20 But do you want to know, O foolish man, that faith without works is dead?

does not have (v. 14)—Again, the verb's form describes someone who continually lacks any external evidence of the faith he routinely claims.

works (v. 14)—This refers to all righteous behavior that conforms to God's revealed Word, but specifically, in the context, to acts of compassion (v. 15).

Can faith save him? (v. 14) —better translated, "Can that kind of faith save?" James is not disputing the importance of faith; rather, he is opposing the notion that saving faith can be a mere intellectual exercise void of a commitment to active obedience. The grammatical form of the question demands a negative answer.

faith by itself ... is dead (v. 17)—Just as professed compassion without action is phony, the kind of faith that is without works is mere empty profession, not genuine saving faith.

someone (v. 18)—Interpreters disagree on (1) whether "someone" is James's humble way of referring to himself or whether it refers to one of James's antagonists who objected to his teaching; and (2) how much of the following passage should be attributed to this antagonist as opposed to James himself. Regardless, James's main point is the same: The only possible evidence of true faith is works.

You believe that there is one God (v. 18)—a clear reference to the passage most familiar to his Jewish readers the shema (Deut. 6:4–5), the most basic doctrine of the Old Testament

demons believe (v. 18)—Even fallen angels affirm the oneness of God and tremble at its implications. Demons are essentially orthodox in their doctrine, but orthodox doctrine by itself is no proof of saving faith. They know the truth about God, Christ, and the Spirit, but hate it and them.

foolish (v. 20)—literally "empty, defective"; the objector's claim of belief is fraudulent, and his faith is a sham

faith without works is dead? (v. 20)—literally "the faith without the works." James is not contrasting two methods of salvation (faith versus works); instead, he contrasts two kinds of faith: living faith that saves and dead faith that does not.

Understanding the Text

2) Is James somehow suggesting that helping the hungry is a prerequisite to salvation? How do you know?

_____

_____

_____

_____

_____

_____

_____

3) What does James say in this passage about a person who claims faith but whose life is void of fruit?

_____

_____

_____

_____

_____

(verses to consider: Matthew 3:7–9; 5:16; 7:15–23; 13:18–23; John 14:21; Hebrews 12:14)

4) What did James mean when he said that the "demons believe"?

_____

_____

_____

_____

_____

_____

_____

(Verses to consider: Matthew 8:29; Mark 5:7; Luke 4:41; Acts 19:15)

Cross-Reference

Read Matthew 25:31–46.

31 *"When the Son of Man comes in His glory, and all the holy angels with Him, then He will sit on the throne of His glory.*

32 *"All the nations will be gathered before Him, and He will separate them one from another, as a shepherd divides his sheep from the goats.*

33 *"And He will set the sheep on His right hand, but the goats on the left.*

34 *"Then the King will say to those on His right hand, 'Come, you blessed of My Father, inherit the kingdom prepared for you from the foundation of the world:*

35 *'for I was hungry and you gave Me food; I was thirsty and you gave Me drink; I was a stranger and you took Me in;*

36 *'I was naked and you clothed Me; I was sick and you visited Me; I was in prison and you came to Me.'*

37 *"Then the righteous will answer Him, saying, 'Lord, when did we see You hungry and feed You, or thirsty and give You drink?*

38 *'When did we see You a stranger and take You in, or naked and clothe You?*

39 *'Or when did we see You sick, or in prison, and come to You?'*

40 *"And the King will answer and say to them, 'Assuredly, I say to you, inasmuch as you did it to one of the least of these My brethren, you did it to Me.'*

41 *"Then He will also say to those on the left hand, 'Depart from Me, you cursed, into the everlasting fire prepared for the devil and his angels:*

42 *'for I was hungry and you gave Me no food; I was thirsty and you gave Me no drink;*

⁴³ *'I was a stranger and you did not take Me in, naked and you did not clothe Me, sick and in prison and you did not visit Me.'*

⁴⁴ *"Then they also will answer Him, saying, 'Lord, when did we see You hungry or thirsty or a stranger or naked or sick or in prison, and did not minister to You?'*

⁴⁵ *"Then He will answer them, saying, 'Assuredly, I say to you, inasmuch as you did not do it to one of the least of these, you did not do it to Me.'*

⁴⁶ *"And these will go away into everlasting punishment, but the righteous into eternal life."*

Exploring the Meaning

5) What does this teaching of the Lord Jesus Christ say about the relationship between faith and works? On what basis does the King in this passage judge His subjects?

_____

_____

_____

_____

_____

6) Read Ephesians 2:8–10. What does this passage say about salvation and works?

_____

_____

_____

_____

_____

_____

7) Read Luke 19:1–10. What does this incident reveal about the transforming nature of saving faith?

_____

_____

_____

_____

_____

(verses to consider: Acts 19:18–19; 1 Thessalonians 1:9)

Summing Up . . .

"All Christians sin (1 John 1:8), but all Christians also obey: 'By this we know that we have come to know Him, if we keep His commandments' (1 John 2:3). Sin and carnality are still present with all believers (Rom. 7:21), but they cannot be the hallmark of one's character (Rom. 6:22)."—*John MacArthur*

Reflecting on the Text

8) Comment on this quote from John MacArthur: "Salvation does not produce immediate perfection, but a new direction. The new disposition that hates sin, loves the Lord, and seeks to know Him and obey His will, begins to manifest itself in behavior."

_____

_____

_____

_____

_____

_____

9) What are the dangers of Christians trying to assess the authenticity of another professing believer's faith?

_____

_____

_____

_____

_____

_____

10) Someone has asked, "If you were tried in a court of law for being a Christian, would there be enough evidence to convict you?" How would you answer this? What undeniable proof of God's saving and sanctifying work do you see in your life?

_____

_____

_____

_____

_____

Recording Your Thoughts

_____

_____

_____

_____

_____

For further study, see the following passages:

Matthew 7:16–18   John 8:30–31   John 15:6
Romans 2:5–10   Ephesians 2:10   2 Timothy 2:19
Titus 1:16   2 Peter 1:3–11   1 John 3:7–10

Faith that Passes the Test!

Opening Thought

1) What is the greatest step of faith you have ever seen someone take?

_____

_____

_____

2) Do you think some Christians have a greater capacity for faith than others? If so, why?

_____

_____

_____

3) When in your life have you taken a great risk and followed what you believed to be God's will, even though some friends and family felt your decision to be foolish? How did you feel in the midst of that time? What finally happened?

_____

_____

_____

4) How can one tell the difference between a faith decision and a foolish decision?

_____

_____

_____

Background of the Passage

In the central passage of this lesson, James contrasts living faith with what he has just described as dead faith (vv. 14–20), saving faith with non-saving faith, productive faith with unproductive faith, godly faith with a kind of faith that is exercised even by demons. In doing so, he does what might be expected, giving living illustrations of living faith. The first is Abraham, revered patriarch and father of the Hebrew people (vv. 21–24). The second is Rahab, a Gentile prostitute (v. 25). The third is a human body, animated by a living spirit (v. 26).

Abraham's and Rahab's justification was not demonstrated by their profession of faith, their worship or ritual, or any other religious activity. In both cases it was demonstrated by putting everything that was dear to them on the line for the Lord, entrusting it to Him without qualification or reservation. They were supremely committed to the Lord, whatever the cost. It is in the vortex of the great plans, decisions, and crossroads of life—where ambitions, hopes, dreams, destinies, and life itself are at stake—that true faith unfailingly reveals itself. Long before Jesus' crucifixion, Abraham and Rahab were willing to take up their crosses, as it were, and follow Him (Mark 8:34). They hated their life in this world in order to keep it in the world to come (John 12:25). Abraham and Rahab stand for all time as examples of those whose living faith passed the test.

Bible Passage

Read James 2:21–26, noting the key words and definitions to the right of the passage.

James 2:21–26

21 *Was not Abraham our father justified by works when he offered Isaac his son on the altar?*

22 *Do you see that faith was working together with his works, and by works faith was made perfect?*

23 *And the Scripture was fulfilled which says, "Abraham believed God, and it was accounted to him for righteousness." And he was called the friend of God.*

justified by works (v. 21)
—This does not contradict Paul's clear teaching that Abraham was justified before God by grace alone through faith alone. For several reasons, James cannot mean that Abraham was constituted righteous before God because of his own good works: (1) James already stressed that salvation is a gracious gift (1:17–18); (2) in the middle of this disputed passage (v. 23),

24 *You see then that a man is justified by works, and not by faith only.*

25 *Likewise, was not Rahab the harlot also justified by works when she received the messengers and sent them out another way?*

26 *For as the body without the spirit is dead, so faith without works is dead also.*

James quoted Genesis 15:6, which forcefully claims that God credited righteousness to Abraham solely on the basis of his faith; and (3) the work that James said justified Abraham was his offering up of Isaac, an event that occurred many years after he first exercised faith and was declared righteous before God. Instead, Abraham's offering of Isaac demonstrated the genuineness of his faith and the reality of his justification before God. James is emphasizing the vindication before others of a man's claim to salvation. His teaching perfectly complements Paul's writings; salvation is determined by faith alone (Eph. 2:8–9) and demonstrated by faithfulness to obey God's will alone (Eph. 2:10).

was made perfect (v. 22)— This refers to bringing something to its end, or to its fullness. Just as a fruit tree has not arrived at its goal until it bears fruit, faith has not reached its end until it demonstrates itself in a righteous life.

the Scripture ... says (v. 23) —quoted from Genesis 15:6

friend of God (v. 23)—so called because of his obedience

Rahab the harlot (v. 25)—The Old Testament records the content of her faith, which was the basis of her justification before God; she demonstrated the reality of her saving faith when, at great personal risk she protected the messengers of God. James did not intend, however, for those words to be a commendation of her occupation or her lying.

justified by works (v. 25)—The Greek verb *dikaioo* (justified) has two general meanings. The first pertains to acquittal, that is, to declaring and treating a person as righteous; that is its meaning in relationship to salvation and is the sense in which Paul almost always uses the term. The second meaning of dikaioo pertains to vindication, or proof of righteousness; it is used in that sense a number of times in the New Testament, in relation to God as well as men. It is this second meaning that is in view in this passage.

Understanding the Text

5) How would you answer the person who argued from James 2:21 that our works or our behavior do play an important role in our salvation?

_____

_____

_____

_____

_____

_____

_____

(Verses to look at: Romans 3:20; Galatians 3:6–11)

6) Can a person be saved apart from Jesus Christ? Were Abraham and Rahab?

_____

_____

_____

_____

_____

_____

(Verses to look at: John 8:56; 14:6; Acts 4:12; Ephesians 2:8–9; Hebrews 5:9; 11:8–10, 13–16, 31)

7) What does "justified" mean?

_____

_____

_____

_____

_____

_____

_____

_____

8) Why is it significant that Abraham was called "the friend of God"? What does this mean?

_____

_____

_____

_____

_____

_____

_____

(Verses to look at: 2 Chronicles 20:7; Isaiah 41:8; John 15:14–15)

9) What was it about Rahab that demonstrated, or vindicated, the presence of saving faith in her life?

_____

_____

_____

_____

_____

_____

_____

(Verses to read: Joshua 2:1–15; 6:17; Hebrews 11:31)

Cross Reference

Romans 4:1–25

¹ *What then shall we say that Abraham our father has found according to the flesh?*

² *For if Abraham was justified by works, he has something to boast about, but not before God.*

³ *For what does the Scripture say? "Abraham believed God, and it was accounted to him for righteousness."*

⁴ *Now to him who works, the wages are not counted as grace but as debt.*

⁵ *But to him who does not work but believes on Him who justifies the ungodly, his faith is accounted for righteousness,*

⁶ *just as David also describes the blessedness of the man to whom God imputes righteousness apart from works:*

⁷ *"Blessed are those whose lawless deeds are forgiven,*
And whose sins are covered;

⁸ *Blessed is the man to whom the Lord shall not impute sin."*

⁹ *Does this blessedness then come upon the circumcised only, or upon the uncircumcised also? For we say that faith was accounted to Abraham for righteousness.*

¹⁰ *How then was it accounted? While he was circumcised, or uncircumcised? Not while circumcised, but while uncircumcised.*

¹¹ *And he received the sign of circumcision, a seal of the righteousness of the faith which he had while still uncircumcised, that he might be the father of all those who believe, though they are uncircumcised, that righteousness might be imputed to them also,*

¹² *and the father of circumcision to those who not only are of the circumcision, but who also walk in the steps of the faith which our father Abraham had while still uncircumcised.*

13 *For the promise that he would be the heir of the world was not to Abraham or to his seed through the law, but through the righteousness of faith.*

14 *For if those who are of the law are heirs, faith is made void and the promise made of no effect,*

15 *because the law brings about wrath; for where there is no law there is no transgression.*

16 *Therefore it is of faith that it might be according to grace, so that the promise might be sure to all the seed, not only to those who are of the law, but also to those who are of the faith of Abraham, who is the father of us all*

17 *(as it is written, "I have made you a father of many nations") in the presence of Him whom he believed—God, who gives life to the dead and calls those things which do not exist as though they did;*

18 *who, contrary to hope, in hope believed, so that he became the father of many nations, according to what was spoken, "So shall your descendants be."*

19 *And not being weak in faith, he did not consider his own body, already dead (since he was about a hundred years old), and the deadness of Sarah's womb.*

20 *He did not waver at the promise of God through unbelief, but was strengthened in faith, giving glory to God,*

21 *and being fully convinced that what He had promised He was also able to perform.*

22 *And therefore "it was accounted to him for righteousness."*

23 *Now it was not written for his sake alone that it was imputed to him,*

24 *but also for us. It shall be imputed to us who believe in Him who raised up Jesus our Lord from the dead,*

25 *who was delivered up because of our offenses, and was raised because of our justification.*

Exploring the Meaning

10) What insights does this passage contribute to your understanding of the relationship between faith and works?

_____

_____

_____

_____

_____

_____

_____

11) Read Hebrews 11:8–19. What does this passage from the chapter often
called "God's Hall of Faith" say about Abraham?

_____

_____

_____

_____

_____

12) Read 2 Corinthians 13:5. In light of the reality of dead faith that often
masquerades as saving faith, what should professing Christians do?

_____

_____

_____

_____

_____

_____

Summing Up . . .

"Abraham was not a perfect man, either in his faith or in his works. After
many years had passed without Sarah's having the promised heir, he took
matters into his own hands, having a son, Ishmael, by Hagar, his wife's maid.

His wavering trust in the Lord led him to commit adultery...In those and other instances, such as his twice lying about Sarah's being his sister (Gen. 12:19; 20:2), his works obviously did not justify him before men.

"But James' point is that, in the overall pattern of his life, Abraham faith-fully vindicated his saving faith through his many good works, above all else by offering Isaac. When a man is justified before God, he will always prove that justification before other men. A man who has been declared and made right-eous will live righteously. Imputed righteousness will manifest practical right-eousness. In the words of John Calvin, 'Faith alone justifies; but the faith that justifies is never alone.'"—*John MacArthur*

Reflecting on the Text

13) In the overall pattern of your life, do your actions vindicate that you do, in fact, possess saving faith? Explain your answer.

_____

_____

_____

_____

_____

_____

14) Why should Rahab's inclusion in this passage be a great encouragement to modern-day Christians?

_____

_____

_____

_____

_____

15) What are some simple but concrete "faith steps" you could take today to force yourself out of your "comfort zone" and into a position where you have no choice but to rely on God?

_____

_____

_____

_____

_____

_____

Recording Your Thoughts

_____

_____

_____

_____

_____

_____

_____

_____

_____

For further study, see the following passages:

Genesis 12:1–7	Genesis 15:6	Genesis 22:9, 12
Matthew 7:21–23	Romans 1:17	Romans 3:24
Ephesians 2:8–10		

Taming the Tongue

Opening Thought

1) It's time for an oral check-up—no, not a dental visit, but an examination of your tongue and mouth. Or more precisely, an inspection of the kind of speech that rolls off your tongue and out of your mouth. Think back over the last week and give yourself a "thumbs up" (i.e., I'm innocent!) or a "thumbs down" (i.e., I'm guilty!) in each of the following categories:

	Thumbs Up	Thumbs Down
Bragging/boasting	_____	_____
Lying	_____	_____
Flattering	_____	_____
Slandering	_____	_____
Gossiping	_____	_____
Verbally abusing others	_____	_____
Cursing	_____	_____
Making off-color remarks	_____	_____
Talking behind another's back	_____	_____
Passing on rumors	_____	_____
Shading the truth	_____	_____
Arguing	_____	_____
Yelling	_____	_____
Being sarcastic or cutting	_____	_____
Teaching questionable "truths"	_____	_____

2) Which of these "sins of the tongue" seem to trip you up most often? Why?

_____

_____

_____

Background of the Passage

The tongue is you in a unique way. It is a tattletale that tells on the heart and discloses the real person. Not only that, but misuse of the tongue is perhaps the easiest way to sin. There are some sins that an individual may not be able to commit simply because he does not have the opportunity. But there are no limits to what one can say, no built-in restraints or boundaries. In Scripture, the tongue is variously described as wicked, deceitful, perverse, filthy, corrupt, flattering, slanderous, gossiping, blasphemous, foolish, boasting, complaining, cursing, contentious, sensual, and vile. And that list is not exhaustive. No wonder God put the tongue in a cage behind the teeth, walled in by the mouth!

Not surprisingly, the tongue is of great concern to James, being mentioned in every chapter of his letter (see 1:19, 26; 2:12; 3:5, 6, 8; 4:11; 5:12). In 3:1–12 he uses the tongue as still another test of living faith, because the genuineness of a person's faith will inevitably be demonstrated by his speech. James personifies the tongue and the mouth as representatives of the depravity and wretchedness of the inner person. The tongue only produces what it is told to produce by the heart, where sin originates (see 1:14–15).

In summary, James teaches that true believers will possess a sanctified tongue, yet they must maintain a sanctified tongue. He gives three compelling reasons for controlling the tongue: its potential to condemn (vv. 1–2a); its power to control (vv. 2b–5a); and its propensity to corrupt (vv. 5b–6).

Bible Passage

Read James 3:1–12, noting the key words and definitions to the right of the passage.

James 3:1–12

¹ *My brethren, let not many of you become teachers, knowing that we shall receive a stricter judgment.*

² *For we all stumble in many things. If anyone does not stumble in word, he is a perfect man, able also to bridle the whole body.*

teachers (v. 1)—This word is translated "master" in the Gospels and refers to a person who functions in an official teaching or preaching capacity

stricter judgment (v. 1)—The word translated "judgment" usually expresses a negative verdict in the New Testament, and here refers to

³ *Indeed, we put bits in horses' mouths that they may obey us, and we turn their whole body.*

⁴ *Look also at ships: although they are so large and are driven by fierce winds, they are turned by a very small rudder wherever the pilot desires.*

⁵ *Even so the tongue is a little member and boasts great things. See how great a forest a little fire kindles!*

⁶ *And the tongue is a fire, a world of iniquity. The tongue is so set among our members that it defiles the whole body, and sets on fire the course of nature; and it is set on fire by hell.*

⁷ *For every kind of beast and bird, of reptile and creature of the sea, is tamed and has been tamed by mankind.*

⁸ *But no man can tame the tongue. It is an unruly evil, full of deadly poison.*

⁹ *With it we bless our God and Father, and with it we curse men, who have been made in the similitude of God.*

¹⁰ *Out of the same mouth proceed blessing and cursing. My brethren, these things ought not to be so.*

¹¹ *Does a spring send forth fresh water and bitter from the same opening?*

¹² *Can a fig tree, my brethren, bear olives, or a grapevine bear figs? Thus no spring yields both salt water and fresh.*

a future judgment: (1) for the unbelieving false teacher, at the second coming (Jude 14, 15); and (2) for the believer, when he is rewarded before Christ (1 Cor. 4:3–5). This is not meant to discourage true teachers, but to warn the prospective teacher of the role's seriousness.

stumble (v. 2)—This refers to sinning, or offending God's Person; the form of the Greek verb emphasizes that everyone continually fails to do what is right.

perfect man (v. 2)—"Perfect" may refer to true perfection, in which case James is saying that, hypothetically, if a human being were able to perfectly control his tongue, he would be a perfect man. Of course, no one is actually immune from sinning with his tongue; so more likely, "perfect" is describing those who are spiritually mature and thus able to control their tongues.

tongue is a fire (v. 6)—Like fire, the tongue's sinful words can spread destruction rapidly, or as its accompanying smoke, those words can permeate and ruin everything around it.

defiles (v. 6)—This means "to pollute or contaminate" (see Mark 7:20; Jude 23).

the course of nature (v. 6) —Better translated "the circle of life," this underscores that the tongue's evil can extend beyond the individual to affect everything in his sphere of influence.

hell (v. 6)—a translation of the Greek word *gehenna* (or valley of Hinnom). In Christ's time this valley that lay southwest of Jerusalem's walls served as the city dump and was known for its constantly burning fire. Jesus used that place to symbolize the eternal place of punishment and torment. To James "hell" conjures up not just the place but the satanic host that will some day inherit it—they use the tongue as a tool for evil.

no man can tame the tongue (v. 8)—Only God, by His power, can do this (see Acts 2:1–11).

bless ... curse (v. 9)—It was traditional for Jews to add "blessed be He" to a mention of God's name; however, the tongue also wishes evil on people made in God's image. This points out the hypocritical inconsistency of the tongue's activities.

made in the similitude of God (v. 9)—Man was made in God's image.

Fountain ... fig tree ... salt water (vv. 11–12)—Three illustrations from nature demonstrate the sinfulness of cursing. The genuine believer will not contradict his profession of faith by the regular use of unwholesome words.

Understanding the Text

3) Who is James addressing when he speaks of "teachers"? Of what does he warn them?

_____

_____

_____

_____

_____

_____

(Verses to look at: Ezekiel 33:7–9; Acts 20:26–27; Ephesians 4:11–12; Hebrews 13:17)

4) According to James, is the root of the problem of evil speech in the mouth/tongue . . . or someplace else?

_____

_____

_____

_____

_____

_____

(Verses to look at: Isaiah 6:5; Matthew 15:11, 16–19; Mark 7:20–23)

5) What types of evils does James say are caused by the tongue?

_____

_____

_____

_____

_____

_____

_____

(Verses to look at: Psalm 5:9; 34:13; 52:4; Proverbs 6:16–17; 26:28)

Cross-Reference

1 Timothy 3:1–7
¹ *This is a faithful saying: If a man desires the position of a bishop, he desires a good work.*
² *A bishop then must be blameless, the husband of one wife, temperate, sober-minded, of good behavior, hospitable, able to teach;*
³ *not given to wine, not violent, not greedy for money, but gentle, not quarrelsome, not covetous;*
⁴ *one who rules his own house well, having his children in submission with all reverence*
⁵ *(for if a man does not know how to rule his own house, how will he take care of the church of God?);*
⁶ *not a novice, lest being puffed up with pride he fall into the same condemnation as the devil.*
⁷ *Moreover he must have a good testimony among those who are outside, lest he fall into reproach and the snare of the devil.*

Exploring the Meaning

6) How does Paul's counsel to Timothy correspond to James's warnings to would-be teachers?

_____

_____

_____

_____

_____

_____

7) Read Genesis 1:26. What truth expressed in this verse should deter us from speaking ill of others?

_____

_____

_____

_____

_____

_____

8) Read Psalm 141:3 and Proverbs 21:23. How do we reconcile these verses with James's claim that "no man can tame the tongue"?

_____

_____

_____

_____

_____

_____

(Verses to look at: Romans 6:12–14; Galatians 5:16–26)

Summing Up . . .

"Nowhere is the relationship between faith and works more evident than in a person's speech. What you are will inevitably be disclosed by what you say. It might be said that a person's speech is a reliable measure of his spiritual temperature, a monitor of the inner human condition. The rabbis spoke of the tongue as an arrow rather than a dagger or sword, because it can wound and kill from a great distance. It can wreak great damage even when far from its victim."—*John MacArthur*

Reflecting on the Text

9) Take a few moments for quiet, Spirit-led introspection. What recent "transgressions of the tongue" are you aware of? What is the solution for these wrong choices? (Hint: see 1 John 1:9.)

_____

_____

_____

_____

_____

_____

10) Are there any people you have publicly slandered or maligned? How can you "fix" this situation? What do you need to do? (Hint: see Matthew 5:21–24.)

_____

_____

_____

_____

_____

_____

_____

11) Using the truths and principles you've learned, in the space below, write down a workable, biblical strategy for avoiding "oral sins" today.

_____

_____

_____

_____

_____

_____

_____

Recording Your Thoughts

_____

_____

_____

_____

_____

_____

For further study, see the following passages:

Psalm 39:1	Psalm 68:19, 35	Proverbs 17:20
Matthew 25:46	Mark 9:43, 45	Romans 3:15
1 Corinthians 12:28	2 Peter 2:14	Jude 23

True Wisdom

Opening Thought

1) Who is the wisest person you've ever known? What made him/her so wise?

_____

_____

_____

_____

_____

2) How much does wisdom count when we are selecting human leaders? Why? What does this say about us?

_____

_____

_____

_____

_____

3) What, in your opinion, is the secret to gaining wisdom?

_____

_____

_____

_____

_____

Background of the Passage

Both Scripture and ancient philosophers placed a premium on wisdom, which, broadly defined, is not simply a matter of possessing factual knowledge but of properly and effectively applying truth to everyday life. The Hebrews especially understood that true wisdom is not intellectual, but behavioral. Thus the biggest fool was one who knew truth and failed to apply it. To the Jews, wisdom was skill in living righteously.

In 3:13, James makes a transition from discussing teachers and the tongue to dealing with wisdom's impact on everyone's life. He supports the truth of Old Testament wisdom literature (Job to Song of Solomon) that wisdom is divided into two realms—man's and God's.

James offers wisdom as still another test of living faith. The kind of wisdom a person possesses will be revealed by the kind of life he lives (v. 13). Those who possess the wisdom of man, the wisdom from below, will demonstrate by their lives that they have no saving relationship with Jesus Christ and no desire to worship, serve, or obey Him (vv. 14–16). Those, on the other hand, who possess genuine saving faith will manifest the wisdom of God, the wisdom from above (vv. 17–18).

Bible Passage

Read James 3:13–18, noting the key words and definitions to the right of the passage.

James 3:13–18

13 *Who is wise and understanding among you? Let him show by good conduct that his works are done in the meekness of wisdom.*

14 *But if you have bitter envy and self-seeking in your hearts, do not boast and lie against the truth.*

15 *This wisdom does not descend from above, but is earthly, sensual, demonic.*

16 *For where envy and self-seeking exist, confusion and every evil thing are there.*

wise and understanding
(v. 13)—Sophos is the common Greek word for speculative knowledge and philosophy, but the Hebrews infused it with the much richer meaning of skillfully applying knowledge to the matter of practical living. The word for "understanding" is used only here in the New Testament and means a specialist or professional who could skillfully apply his expertise to practical situations. James is asking who is truly skilled in the art of living.

17 But the wisdom that is from above is first pure, then peaceable, gentle, willing to yield, full of mercy and good fruits, without partiality and without hypocrisy.

18 Now the fruit of righteousness is sown in peace by those who make peace.

meekness (v. 13)—Also rendered "gentleness," it is the opposite of arrogance and self-promotion; the Greeks described it as power under control.

wisdom (v. 13)—the kind that comes only from God

bitter envy (v. 14)—The Greek term for "bitter" was used of undrinkable water; when combined with "envy" it defines a harsh, resentful attitude toward others.

self-seeking (v. 14)—Sometimes translated "strife," it refers to selfish ambition that engenders antagonism and factionalism. The Greek word came to describe anyone who entered politics for selfish reasons and sought to achieve his agenda at any cost (i.e., even if that meant trampling on others).

from above (v. 15)—Self-centered wisdom that is consumed with personal ambition is not from God.

earthly, sensual, demonic (v. 15)—a description of man's wisdom as: (1) limited to earth; (2) characterized by humanness, frailty, an unsanctified heart, and an unredeemed spirit; and (3) generated by Satan's forces

confusion (v. 16)—This is the disorder that results from the instability and chaos of human wisdom.

every evil thing (v. 16)—literally "every worthless [or vile] work"; this denotes things that are not so much intrinsically evil as they are simply good for nothing

pure (v. 17)—This refers to spiritual integrity and moral sincerity; every genuine Christian has this kind of heart motivation.

peaceable (v. 17)—means "peace loving" or "peace promoting"

gentle (v. 17)—This word is difficult to translate, but most nearly means a character trait of sweet reasonableness. Such a person will submit to all kinds of mistreatment and difficulty with an attitude of kind, courteous, patient humility, without any thought of hatred or revenge (see Matt. 5:10, 11).

willing to yield (v. 17)—The original term described someone who was teachable, compliant, easily persuaded, and who willingly submitted to military discipline or moral and legal standards; for believers, it defines obedience to God's standards (see Matt. 5:3–5).

full of mercy (v. 17)—the gift of showing concern for those who suffer pain and hardship, and the ability to forgive quickly (see Matt. 5:7)

without partiality (v. 17)—The Greek word occurs only here in the New Testament and denotes a consistent, unwavering person who is undivided in his commitment and conviction and does not make unfair distinctions.

fruit of righteousness (v. 18)—good works that result from salvation (see v. 17)

those who make peace (v. 18)—Righteousness flourishes in a climate of spiritual peace.

Understanding the Text

4) How is godly wisdom described and defined in this passage?

_____

_____

_____

_____

_____

_____

_____

_____

(Verses to look at: Job 28; Psalm 104:24; Proverbs 1:7; Daniel 1:17; Romans 11:33)

5) What did James mean when he referred to the "meekness of wisdom" (v. 13)?

_____

_____

_____

_____

_____

_____

_____

_____

(Verses to look at: Matthew 5:5; Galatians 5:22–23)

6) What did James say about the nature and source (as well as the danger) of so-called human wisdom?

_____

_____

_____

_____

_____

_____

_____

(Verses to look at: 1 Corinthians 1:18–31; 2:6–16)

7) What does it mean that God's wisdom is "pure" (v. 17)?

_____

_____

_____

_____

_____

_____

_____

_____

(Verses to look at: Psalm 24:3–4; Matthew 5:8)

8) What are the results of a life that is marked and governed by God's wisdom?

_____

_____

_____

_____

_____

_____

_____

(Verses to look at: Matthew 5:6; Galatians 5:22–23; Philippians 1:11)

Cross-Reference

Proverbs 2:1–7
¹ *My son, if you receive my words,*
  And treasure my commands within you,
² *So that you incline your ear to wisdom,*
  And apply your heart to understanding;
³ *Yes, if you cry out for discernment,*
  And lift up your voice for understanding,
⁴ *If you seek her as silver,*
  And search for her as for hidden treasures;
⁵ *Then you will understand the fear of the* LORD*,*
  And find the knowledge of God.
⁶ *For the* LORD *gives wisdom;*

From His mouth come knowledge and understanding;
⁷ *He stores up sound wisdom for the upright;*
He is a shield to those who walk uprightly.

Exploring the Meaning

9) What does this passage, penned by King Solomon, say about the nature of wisdom?

_____

_____

_____

_____

_____

_____

_____

10) Read Colossians 2:3. What does this passage say about Christ and wisdom?

_____

_____

_____

_____

_____

_____

_____

_____

Summing Up . . .

"If a person professes saving faith in Jesus Christ and claims to have wisdom from God, but has a heart that is proud, arrogant, and self-centered and lives a life that is worldly, sensual, and self-serving, his claims to salvation are false. He is lying against the truth."—*John MacArthur*

Reflecting on the Text

11) How can a person tell if the wisdom he/she is receiving is man's or God's?

_____

_____

_____

_____

_____

_____

_____

12) To what degree does the world's wisdom hold sway over your thoughts, opinions, and values? Why?

_____

_____

_____

_____

_____

_____

_____

13) What are some concrete ways a Christian can acquire God's wisdom? Try to list ten. Circle the ones you regularly practice. Put a check mark by the activities that need to become part of your daily experience.

_____

_____

_____

_____

_____

_____

_____

_____

14) A young Christian comes to you and says: "I just read in Proverbs that we're to seek after wisdom in the same way that someone might eagerly search for silver or gold. I don't seem to find within myself that kind of urgency. How can I develop such a hunger for wisdom?"

How would you respond? What can you do today to become more passionate about pursuing God's wisdom?

_____

_____

_____

_____

_____

_____

_____

_____

Recording Your Thoughts

_____

_____

_____

_____

_____

_____

_____

_____

_____

_____

_____

_____

_____

_____

_____

_____

_____

_____

_____

_____

_____

For further study, see the following passages:

Psalm 51:7	Psalm 111:10	Proverbs 3:19–20
Daniel 2:20–23	Matthew 5:9	Romans 12:8
1 Corinthians 1:30	Ephesians 3:10	James 1:5

Worldliness!

Opening Thought

1) How would/do most Christians define "worldliness"? Give some examples of activities that are typically viewed as "worldly."

_____

_____

_____

_____

_____

2) What's the worst church fight or church split you've ever witnessed? What was the cause?

_____

_____

_____

_____

_____

3) How bad is gossip in your church? Why?

_____

_____

_____

_____

Background of the Passage

Like a spiritual barometer or a checklist for the soul, the New Testament Epistle of James was written for professed Christians to test their faith for its genuiness.

Intensely practical and down-to-earth, James examines a number of everyday behaviors that can serve either to authenticate one's claim to conversion or highlight the absence of true saving faith. After addressing the issues of the tongue and of wisdom in chapter 3, James begins chapter 4 with another test of genuine Christian faith—one's attitude toward the world. The central truth in this passage is, "Friendship with the world is hostility toward God" (4:4). James argues persuasively that genuine spiritual life and faithful Christian living involve separation from the world and all its countless contaminations. Conversely, a continuing, habitual friendship with the world is grounded in human wisdom and is evidence of unbelief. Such a lifestyle invariably leads to personal conflict—both interpersonal and intrapersonal (4:1–6).

In case any reader realizes that he/she has been deceived, in verses 7–10 James offers unbelievers an invitation to saving faith. This passage admonishes readers to humbly put away any remaining vestiges of their former worldly living that continue to impede their spiritual lives. The primary emphasis here is on those who claim to be saved but are not.

Finally, having shown that the mark of a true believer is humility (v. 10), James reveals one practical way in which humility is violated and pride revealed, through the blasphemous sin of defaming others (vv. 11–12).

Bible Passage

Read James 4:1–12, noting the key words and definitions to the right of the passage.

James 4:1–12

1 *Where do wars and fights come from among you? Do they not come from your desires for pleasure that war in your members?*

2 *You lust and do not have. You murder and covet*

wars and fights ... among you (v. 1)—These are between people in the church, not internal conflict in individual people. "Wars" speaks of the conflict in general; "fights" of its specific manifestations. Discord in the church is not by God's design, but

and cannot obtain. *You fight and war. Yet you do not have because you do not ask.*

³ *You ask and do not receive, because you ask amiss, that you may spend it on your pleasures.*

⁴ *Adulterers and adulteresses! Do you not know that friendship with the world is enmity with God? Whoever therefore wants to be a friend of the world makes himself an enemy of God.*

⁵ *Or do you think that the Scripture says in vain, "The Spirit who dwells in us yearns jealously"?*

⁶ *But He gives more grace. Therefore He says:*
"God resists the proud,
But gives grace to the humble."

⁷ *Therefore submit to God. Resist the devil and he will flee from you.*

⁸ *Draw near to God and He will draw near to you. Cleanse your hands, you sinners; and purify your hearts, you double-minded.*

⁹ *Lament and mourn and weep! Let your laughter be turned to mourning and your joy to gloom.*

¹⁰ *Humble yourselves in the sight of the Lord, and He will lift you up.*

¹¹ *Do not speak evil of one another, brethren. He who speaks evil of a brother and judges his brother, speaks evil of the law and judges the law. But if you judge the law, you are not a doer of the law but a judge.*

¹² *There is one Lawgiver, who is able to save and to destroy. Who are you to judge another?*

results from the mix of tares (false believers) and wheat (truly redeemed people) that make up the church.

desires (v. 1)—The Greek word (from which the English word "hedonism" derives) always has a negative connotation in the New Testament; the passionate desires for worldly pleasures that mark unbelievers (1:14) are the internal source of the external conflict in the church. Cf. 1:14–15.

your members (v. 1)—not church members, but bodily members (see Rom. 6:13). James, like Paul, uses "members" to speak of sinful, fallen human nature (see Rom. 6:19); unbelievers (who are in view here) fight (unsuccess-fully) against the evil desires they cannot control.

murder (v. 2)—the ultimate result of thwarted desires; James had in mind actual murder, and the gamut of sins (hate, anger, bitter-ness) leading up to it. The picture is of unbelievers so driven by their uncontrollable evil desires that they will fight to the death to fulfill them.

you do not ask (v. 2)—True joy, peace, happiness, meaning, hope, and fulfillment in life come only from God; unbelievers, however, are unwilling to ask for them on His terms—they refuse to submit to God or acknowledge their dependence on Him.

amiss (v. 3)—This refers to act-ing in an evil manner, motivated by personal gratification and self-ish desire; unbelievers seek things for their own pleasures, not the honor and glory of God.

Adulterers and adulteresses! (v. 4)—This metaphorical descrip-tion of spiritual unfaithfulness would have been especially famil-iar to James's Jewish readers, since the Old Testament often describes unfaithful Israel as a spiritual harlot (see Hosea 9:1). James has in view professing Christians, outwardly associated with the church, but holding a deep affection for the evil world system.

friendship (v. 4)—Appearing only here in the New Testament, the Greek word describes love in the sense of a strong emotional attachment; those with a deep and intimate longing for the things of the world give evidence that they are not redeemed.

enmity with God (v. 4)—the necessary corollary to friendship with the world; the sobering truth that unbelievers are God's enemies is taught throughout Scripture (see Deut. 32:41–43)

Scripture says (v. 5)—a common New Testament way of introducing an Old Testament quote (John 19:37; Rom. 4:3; 9:17; 10:11; 11:2; Gal. 4:30; 1 Tim. 5:18). The quote that follows, however, is not found as such in the Old Testament but it is a composite of general Old Testament teaching.

The Spirit ... yearns jealously (v. 5)—This difficult phrase is best understood by seeing the "spirit" as a reference not to the Holy Spirit, but to the human spirit, and translating the phrase "yearns jealously" in the negative sense of "lusts to envy." James's point is that an unbelieving person's spirit (inner person) is bent on evil; those who think otherwise defy the biblical diagnosis of fallen human nature; and those who live in worldly lusts give evidence that their faith is not genuine (see Rom. 8:5–11; 1 Cor. 2:14).

more grace (v. 6)—The only ray of hope in man's spiritual darkness is the sovereign grace of God, which alone can rescue man from his propensity to lust for evil things. That God gives "more grace" shows that His grace is greater than the power of sin, the flesh, the world, and Satan (see Rom. 5:20). The Old Testament quote (from Prov. 3:34) reveals who obtains God's grace—the humble, not the proud enemies of God. The word "humble" does not define a special class of Christians, but encompasses all believers (see Is. 57:15; Matt. 18:3, 4).

submit (v. 7)—Literally "to line up under," the word was used of soldiers under the authority of their commander. In the New Testament, it describes Jesus' submission to His parents' authority (Luke 2:51), submission to human government (Rom. 13:1), the church's submission to Christ (Eph. 5:24), and servants' submission to their masters (Titus 2:9; 1 Pet. 2:18). James used the word to describe a willing, conscious submission to God's authority as sovereign ruler of the universe. A truly humble person will give his allegiance to God, obey His commands, and follow His leadership.

Resist the devil and he will flee from you (v. 7)—the flip side of the first command. "Resist" literally means "take your stand against". All people are either under the lordship of Christ or the lordship of Satan; there is no middle ground. Those who transfer their allegiance from Satan to God will find that Satan "will flee from" them since he is a defeated foe.

Draw near (v. 8)—pursue an intimate love relationship with God. The concept of drawing near to God was associated originally with the Levitical priests (Lev. 10:3; Ezek. 44:13), but eventually came to describe anyone's approach to God. Salvation involves more than submitting to God and resisting the devil; the redeemed heart longs for communion with God (Ps. 42:1–2).

Cleanse your hands (v. 8)—The Old Testament priests had to ceremonially wash their hands before approaching God, and sinners (a term used only for unbelievers) who would approach Him must recognize and confess their sin.

purify your hearts (v. 8)—Cleansing the hands symbolizes external behavior; this phrase refers to the inner thoughts, motives, and desires of the heart.

Lament (v. 9)—be afflicted, wretched, and miserable; this is the state of those truly broken over their sin

mourn (v. 9)—God will not turn away a heart broken and contrite over sin (2 Cor. 7:10); mourning is the inner response to such brokenness.

weep (v. 9)—the outward manifestation of inner sorrow over sin

laughter (v. 9)—Used only here in the New Testament, the word signifies the flippant laughter of those foolishly indulging in worldly pleasures. The picture is of people who give no thought to God, life, death, sin, judgment, or holiness. James calls on such people to mourn over their sin (see Luke 18:13–14).

speak evil (v. 11)—This means to slander or defame. James does not forbid confronting those in sin, which is elsewhere commanded in Scripture (Matt. 18:15–17; Titus 1:13; 2:15; 3:10); rather, he condemns careless, derogatory, critical, slanderous accusations against others (see Ps. 50:20; Prov. 10:18; Rom. 1:29; Titus 2:3).

speaks evil of a brother ... speaks evil of the law (v. 11)—Those who speak evil of other believers set themselves up as judges and condemn them (see 2:4). They thereby defame and disregard God's law, which expressly forbids such slanderous condemnation.

judges the law (v. 11)—By refusing to submit to the law, slanderers place themselves above it as its judges.

one Lawgiver (v. 12)—God, who gave the law (see Is. 33:22); He alone has the authority to save those who repent from its penalty and destroy those who refuse to repent

Understanding the Text

4) Why is James so intolerant of conflict in the church? What are the most common causes of this infighting?

_____

_____

_____

_____

_____

(Verses to look at: John 17:20–21; 2 Corinthians 12:20; Ephesians 2:3; 2 Timothy 3:2–5)

5) Why does James address some of his readers as "adulterers and adulteresses"? What does this phrase mean?

_____

_____

_____

_____

_____

_____

6) What should be the Christian's relationship with the world?

_____

_____

_____

_____

(Verses to look at: 1 John 2:15–17)

7) What does it mean to be at enmity with God (v. 4)?

_____

_____

_____

_____

(Verses to look at: Psalm 21:8; Isaiah 42:13; Nahum 1:2, 8; Luke 19:27; Romans 5:10; 1 Corinthians 15:25)

8) What does James say is the bent of an unbelieving person's spirit (v. 5)?

_____

_____

_____

_____

(Verses to look at: Genesis 6:5; Proverbs 21:10; Jeremiah 17:9; Mark 7:21–23)

9) Why is James so adamant about not slandering others? Does this mean that believers are forbidden to confront overt sin in others?

_____

_____

_____

_____

(Verses to look at: Proverbs 10:18; 11:9; 1 Corinthians 4:14; 2 Corinthians 12:20; Ephesians 4:31; Colossians 1:28; 2 Timothy 3:3; Titus 2:3)

Cross Reference

Read Psalm 63:1–11.
A Psalm of David when he was in the wilderness of Judah.
¹ *O God, You are my God;*
   Early will I seek You;
   My soul thirsts for You;
   My flesh longs for You
   In a dry and thirsty land
   Where there is no water.
² *So I have looked for You in the sanctuary,*
   To see Your power and Your glory.
³ *Because Your lovingkindness is better than life,*
   My lips shall praise You.
⁴ *Thus I will bless You while I live;*
   I will lift up my hands in Your name.
⁵ *My soul shall be satisfied as with marrow and fatness,*
   And my mouth shall praise You with joyful lips.
⁶ *When I remember You on my bed,*
   I meditate on You in the night watches.
⁷ *Because You have been my help,*
   Therefore in the shadow of Your wings I will rejoice.
⁸ *My soul follows close behind You;*
   Your right hand upholds me.

⁹ But those who seek my life, to destroy it,
  Shall go into the lower parts of the earth.
¹⁰ They shall fall by the sword;
  They shall be a portion for jackals.
¹¹ But the king shall rejoice in God;
  Everyone who swears by Him shall glory;
  But the mouth of those who speak lies shall be stopped.

Exploring the Meaning

10) What does this passage teach about drawing near to God? In what ways is this desire the mark of a true believer?

_____

_____

_____

_____

_____

(Verses to look at: Psalm 27:8; 73:28; Hebrews 4:16)

11) Read Psalm 24:3–4. What are the prerequisites to drawing near to God?

_____

_____

_____

_____

_____

(Verses to look at: Ezekiel 18:31; 36:25–26; 2 Timothy 2:22; 1 Peter 1:22)

12) Read John 8:44. What is the relationship between unbelievers and Satan?

_____

_____

_____

_____

_____

(Verses to look at: Ephesians 2:2; 1 John 3:8; 5:19)

Summing Up . . .

"Friendship with the world and friendship with God are mutually exclusive....Christians have a nature so utterly distinct from the lovers of the world, the followers of Satan, that they should never entertain any of the ways or hold any of the loyalties that characterize unbelievers....For believers to pursue worldly things goes against the grain of their new nature and they cannot be comfortable or satisfied until they renounce those things and return to their first love."—*John MacArthur*

Reflecting on the Text

13) Where do your affections lie? In what ways are you too enamored with the things of this world? What do you need to do?

_____

_____

_____

_____

_____

14) In verses 2 and 3 James addresses the issue of improper motives in the prayers of unbelievers. Examine your own prayer life. What percentage of your prayer life is focused on selfish desires? How can you change this?

_____

_____

_____

_____

_____

15) James denounced the destructive sin of defaming others. Why is gossip, then, such an "acceptable" sin in the eyes of many believers? How careful are you when speaking about others? Spend a few minutes carefully meditating on James 4:11–12. What do you sense God telling you in this passage?

_____

_____

_____

_____

_____

Recording Your Thoughts

_____

_____

_____

_____

_____

_____

For further study, see the following passages:

Genesis 8:21	Psalm 68:21	Psalm 75:6
Psalm 84:2	Psalm 101:5	Psalm 110:1–2
Psalm 140:11	Psalm 143:6	Proverbs 16:28
Proverbs 17:9	Proverbs 26:20	Isaiah 6:5
Isaiah 66:2	Jeremiah 3:1, 6, 8–9	Hosea 4:15
Matthew 5:4	Matthew 10:38	Matthew 22:37
Matthew 23:12	Mark 14:72	Romans 7:5, 23
Romans 8:5–7	1 Corinthians 1:10	2 Corinthians 6:14–18
Titus 3:2	Hebrews 7:19	Hebrews 10:22
1 Peter 5:5	Jude 18	

Responding to the Will of God

Opening Thought

1) How would you define the phrase "the will of God"?

_____

_____

_____

2) What are some of the more common ways Christians attempt to discern God's will?

_____

_____

_____

3) What are some examples from your own life, or from the life of someone you know, in which a certain decision was initially deemed to be "the will of God" but later proved to be a colossal mistake? What happened?

_____

_____

_____

4) How do *you* go about determining God's will for your life? Why?

_____

_____

_____

Background of the Passage

For James, doing the will of God identifies another test of genuine saving faith. True Christians are characterized as "doing the will of God from the heart" (Ephesians 6:6). They joyfully, willingly pray, "Your kingdom come, Your will be done" (Matthew 6:10). The apostle Paul's delight in God's law (Romans 7:22) is another way of expressing the same attitude.

On the other hand, a constant disregard for or lack of interest in God's will is a certain mark of the presence of pride—the ugly sin also underlying conflict, worldliness, and slander (4:1–12). To disregard God's will is tantamount to saying, "I am the sovereign ruler of my own life." Such a prideful attitude is antithetical to saving faith. As James has already pointed out, "God is opposed to the proud, but gives grace to the humble" (4:6). Those who refuse to submit to God's will give evidence that their lives have not been transformed by His saving grace.

True to the pattern he has followed throughout his epistle, James takes a practical approach to the issue of responding to God's will. In a fascinating passage built around the seemingly mundane illustration of businessmen's plans, James gives significant insights into how people respond to God's will. In so doing, he presents three negative responses and one positive one.

Bible Passage

Read James 4:13–17, noting the key words and definitions to the right of the passage.

James 4:13–17

13 Come now, you who say, "Today or tomorrow we will go to such and such a city, spend a year there, buy and sell, and make a profit";

14 whereas you do not know what will happen tomorrow. For what is your life? It is even a vapor that appears for a little time and then vanishes away.

15 Instead you ought to say, "If the Lord wills, we shall live and do this or that."

"Today or tomorrow..." (v. 13)
—James does not condemn wise business planning, but rather planning that leaves out God; the people so depicted are practical atheists, living their lives and making their plans as if God did not exist. Such conduct is inconsistent with genuine saving faith, which submits to God.

know what will happen (v. 14)—James exposes the presumptuous folly of the practical

¹⁶ *But now you boast in your arrogance. All such boasting is evil.*

¹⁷ *Therefore, to him who knows to do good and does not do it, to him it is sin.*

atheists he condemned in v. 13. They do not know what the future holds for them; God alone knows the future.

vapor (v. 14)—This refers either to a puff of smoke or one's breath that appears for a moment in cold air. It stresses the transitory nature of life (see 1:10; Job 7:6–7).

the Lord wills (v. 15)—The true Christian submits his plans to the lordship of Christ (see v. 7).

boasting (v. 16)—arrogant bragging about their anticipated business accomplishments

sin (v. 17)—The implication is that they also did what they shouldn't do; sins of omission lead directly to sins of commission.

Understanding the Text

5) How does James characterize our lives (i.e. the length of our lives)? Why is this significant?

_____

_____

_____

_____

_____

_____

_____

_____

_____

(Verses to look at: Job 9:25–26; Psalm 39:5, 11; 62:9; 90:5–6, 10

6) Why does James insist that we preface our plans by saying, "If the Lord wills..."? What does this mindset indicate?

_____

_____

_____

_____

_____

_____

_____

_____

(Verses to look at: Proverbs 19:21; Acts 18:21; Romans 1:10; 1 Corinthians 4:19)

7) How does a concern for the will of God demonstrate our belief in His sovereignty?

_____

_____

_____

_____

_____

_____

_____

_____

(Verses to look at: Deuteronomy 32:39; Job 12:9–10; Psalm 104:29; Hebrews 9:27)

8) According to James, what lies behind the reasoning that excludes God and His will?

_____

_____

_____

_____

_____

_____

_____

_____

Cross-Reference

Read Luke 12:13–21.

¹³ *Then one from the crowd said to Him, "Teacher, tell my brother to divide the inheritance with me."*

¹⁴ *But He said to him, "Man, who made Me a judge or an arbitrator over you?"*

¹⁵ *And He said to them, "Take heed and beware of covetousness, for one's life does not consist in the abundance of the things he possesses."*

¹⁶ *Then He spoke a parable to them, saying: "The ground of a certain rich man yielded plentifully.*

¹⁷ *"And he thought within himself, saying, 'What shall I do, since I have no room to store my crops?'*

¹⁸ *"So he said, 'I will do this: I will pull down my barns and build greater, and there I will store all my crops and my goods.*

¹⁹ *'And I will say to my soul, "Soul, you have many goods laid up for many years; take your ease; eat, drink, and be merry." '*

²⁰ *"But God said to him, 'Fool! This night your soul will be required of you; then whose will those things be which you have provided?'*

²¹ *"So is he who lays up treasure for himself, and is not rich toward God."*

Exploring the Meaning

9) What does this parable of Christ teach about priorities? about wealth? about certainties in life?

_____

_____

_____

_____

_____

_____

_____

_____

10) Read Proverbs 27:1. Why is it foolish to presume on the future?

_____

_____

_____

_____

_____

_____

_____

11) Read Isaiah 46:9–10. What does this passage say about God and the future?

_____

_____

_____

_____

_____

_____

_____

_____

_____

Summing Up . . .

"The Scriptures give many marks of a true Christian, such as love for God, repentance from sin, humility, devotion to God's glory, prayer, love for others, separation from the world, growth, and obedience. But nothing more clearly summarizes the character of a genuine believer than a desire to do the will of God."—*John MacArthur*

Reflecting on the Text

12) What are some things which are clearly the will of God?

_____

_____

_____

_____

_____

_____

_____

_____

_____

(Verses to look at: Ephesians 5:17–21; 1 Thessalonians 4:3–8; 1 Peter 2:13–15; 1 Peter 3:17)

13) Ponder your approach to a typical day. How much does God and His will figure into your plans? Is His kingdom and His righteousness (Matthew 6:33) foremost in your thoughts? Or are spiritual realities shoved into the margins of your life as an afterthought?

_____

_____

_____

_____

_____

_____

_____

14) How can you become more concerned about and focused on knowing and doing the will of God?

_____

_____

_____

_____

_____

_____

_____

_____

15) Someone has said that about 90 percent of God's will for our lives is already revealed in the Bible. In other words, God has already unveiled what should be the primary direction of our lives, and as we obey those broad principles, He makes the details clear.

If this is true, then a careful study and knowledge of Scripture is imperative for believers. Consider your own habits in the area of Biblical instruction. How much time per week do you spend in:

_____ hearing God's Word read/preached/taught?
_____ reading God's Word?
_____ studying God's Word (i.e., digging deeper into specific passages)?
_____ memorizing God's Word?
_____ meditating on God's Word (i.e., letting the truths of Scripture permeate deeply into your heart and mind)?

16) As you ponder your responses to that question, what two specific changes do you need to make this week?

_____

_____

_____

_____

_____

_____

_____

Recording Your Thoughts

_____

_____

_____

_____

_____

_____

_____

_____

_____

_____

For further study, see the following passages:

Job 14:1–2	Psalm 89:47	Acts 21:14
Romans 15:32	1 Corinthians 16:7	Titus 2:11–12
2 Peter 3:9		

Riches, Trials, and Swearing

Opening Thought

1) Some years ago, a popular Christian teacher insisted that it was an overt sin for North American believers to drive expensive foreign cars when people (and especially fellow Christians) around the world were starving to death. Others have since followed suit—looking unfavorably on Western Christians who live in luxurious homes or who spend extravagantly on clothes or vacations.

Are these advocates of frugal living right or wrong? Why or why not? In what ways is wealth (and our stewardship of it) a "relative" issue?

_____

_____

_____

_____

_____

2) Some of the fastest-growing churches in Christendom are those which advocate the so-called health and wealth gospel. In extreme forms, this teaching says that Christianity is intended to be a life-long time of physical blessing, which is typically defined as peace and prosperity in this world here and now.

Why is this message so popular? Is it biblical? Why or why not?

_____

_____

_____

3) In courtrooms every day, witnesses place their hand on the Bible and swear to tell the truth, the whole truth, and nothing but the truth. Is this a Christian practice or not? Why do you say that?

_____

_____

_____

_____

_____

Background of the Passage

As noted throughout this study, James's goal was to present various tests of genuine saving faith, tests which validate or invalidate one's claim to be a Christian. Building on the teaching of our Lord, as he often does, James presents additional tests in chapter 5. The first has to do with how one views money.

The first six verses of chapter 5 form a strong rebuke—the strongest in the entire epistle. James's blistering, scathing denunciation condemns those who profess to worship God but in fact worship money. His rebuke of the wicked wealthy is in keeping with the tradition of the Old Testament prophets. He calls on them to examine the true state of their hearts in light of how they feel about wealth.

In verses 7–11 he shifts his focus from the persecutors (i.e., the wicked rich) to the persecuted, moving from condemning the faithless wealthy to comforting the faithful poor. James instructs the suffering poor as to what attitude they are to have in the midst of persecution. The theme of this section is defining how to be patient in trials.

Verse 12 touches on another custom during biblical times, that of swearing oaths. This practice had become an issue in the church, particularly since swearing oaths was an integral part of Jewish culture and Jewish believers comprised a large segment of the early church. To encourage believers to be distinctive in the matter of speaking the truth, James issued the command to stop swearing oaths.

Bible Passage

Read James 5:1–12, noting the key words and definitions to the right of the passage.

James 5:1–12

¹ *Come now, you rich, weep and howl for your miseries that are coming upon you!*

² *Your riches are corrupted, and your garments are moth-eaten.*

³ *Your gold and silver are corroded, and their corrosion will be a witness against you and will eat your flesh like fire. You have heaped up treasure in the last days.*

⁴ *Indeed the wages of the laborers who mowed your fields, which you kept back by fraud, cry out; and the cries of the reapers have reached the ears of the Lord of Sabaoth.*

⁵ *You have lived on the earth in pleasure and luxury; you have fattened your hearts as in a day of slaughter.*

⁶ *You have condemned, you have murdered the just; he does not resist you.*

⁷ *herefore be patient, brethren, until the coming of the Lord. See how the farmer waits for the precious fruit of the earth, waiting patiently for it until it receives the early and latter rain.*

⁸ *You also be patient. Establish your hearts, for the coming of the Lord is at hand.*

⁹ *Do not grumble against one another, brethren, lest you be condemned. Behold, the Judge is standing at the door!*

¹⁰ *My brethren, take the prophets, who spoke in the name of the Lord, as an example of suffering and patience.*

rich (v. 1)—those with more than they need to live. James condemns them not for being wealthy, but for misusing their resources. Unlike the believing rich in Timothy's congregation (1 Tim. 6:17–19), these are the wicked wealthy who profess Christian faith and have associated themselves with the church, but whose real god is money. For prostituting the goodness and generosity of God, they can anticipate only divine punishment (v. 5).

corrupted … moth-eaten … corroded (vv. 2–3)—James points out the folly of hoarding food, expensive clothing, or money—all of which is subject to decay, theft, fire, or other forms of loss.

last days (v. 3)—the period between Christ's first and second comings; James rebukes the rich for living as if Jesus were never coming back

wages … you kept back (v. 4)—The rich had gained some of their wealth by oppressing and defrauding their day laborers—a practice strictly forbidden in the Old Testament (see Lev. 19:13; Deut. 24:14–15).

the Lord of Sabaoth (v. 4)—an untranslated Hebrew word meaning "hosts"; the One who hears the cries of the defrauded laborers, James warns, is the Lord of

11 *Indeed we count them blessed who endure. You have heard of the perseverance of Job and seen the end intended by the Lord—that the Lord is very compassionate and merciful.*

12 *But above all, my brethren, do not swear, either by heaven or by earth or with any other oath. But let your "Yes," be "Yes," and your "No," "No," lest you fall into judgment.*

hosts (a name for God used frequently in the Old Testament), the com-mander of the armies of heaven (angels); the Bible teaches that angels will be involved in the judgment of unbelievers (Matt. 13:39–41, 49; 16:27; 25:31; 2 Thess. 1:7–8)

pleasure and luxury (v. 5) —After robbing their workers to accumulate their wealth, the rich indulged themselves in an extravagant lifestyle. "Pleasure" has the connotation of wanton pleasure. "Luxury" leads to vice when a person becomes consumed with the pursuit of pleasure, since a life without self-denial soon becomes out of control in every area.

a day of slaughter (v. 5)—Like fattened cattle ready to be slaughtered, the rich that James condemns had indulged themselves to the limit; this is a vivid depiction of divine judgment, in keeping with the metaphor likening the overindulgent rich to fattened cattle.

condemned ... murdered (v. 6)—This describes the next step in the sinful progression of the rich. Hoarding led to fraud, which led to self-indulgence; finally, that overindulgence has consumed the rich to the point that they will do anything to sustain their lifestyle. "Condemned" comes from a word meaning "to sentence"; the implication is that the rich were using the courts to commit judicial murder (see 2:6).

patient (v. 7)—The word emphasizes patience with people (see 1 Thess. 5:14), rather than in trials or difficult circumstances (as in 1:3); specifically, James has in mind patience with the oppressive rich.

the coming (v. 7)—the second coming of Christ; realizing the glory that awaits them at Christ's return should motivate believers to patiently endure mistreatment

the early and latter rain (v. 7)—The "early" rain falls in Israel during October and November and softens the ground for planting; the "latter" rain falls in March and April, immediately before the spring harvest. Just as the farmer waits patiently from the early rain to the latter for his crop to ripen, so must Christians patiently wait for the Lord's return (see Gal. 6:9; 2 Tim. 4:8; Titus 2:13).

Establish your hearts (v. 8)—a call for resolute, firm courage and commitment; James exhorts those about to collapse under the weight of persecution to shore up their hearts with the hope of the second coming

at hand (v. 8)—The imminency of Christ's return is a frequent theme in the New Testament.

Do not grumble ... the Judge is standing at the door! (v. 9)—James pictured Christ as a judge about to open the doors to the courtroom and convene His court. Knowing that the strain of persecution could lead to grumbling, James cautioned his readers against that sin, lest they forfeit their full reward.

the perseverance of Job (v. 11)—Job is the classic example of a man who patiently endured suffering and was blessed by God for his persevering faith; James reassured his readers that God had a purpose for their suffering, just as He did for Job's.

compassionate and merciful (v. 11)—Remembering the Lord's character is a great comfort in suffering. The Scriptures repeatedly affirm His compassion and mercy (see Psalms 25:6; 103:8, 13; 116:5; 136:1; 145:8).

above all (v. 12)—or "especially"; as he has done repeatedly in his epistle, James stressed that a person's speech provides the most revealing glimpse of his spiritual condition (see 1:26; 2:12; 3:2–11; 4:11)

do not swear ... any other oath (v. 12)—As Jesus did before him (Matt. 5:33–36; 23:16–22), James condemned the contemporary Jewish practice of swearing false, evasive, deceptive oaths by everything other than the name of the Lord (which alone was considered binding).

"Yes" be "Yes" (v. 12)—Again echoing Jesus, James called for straightforward, honest, plain speech; to speak otherwise is to invite God's judgment.

Understanding the Text

4) What characteristic of the wealthy was James decrying? Why was he so harsh in his rebuke?

_____

_____

_____

_____

_____

_____

_____

_____

_____

_____

(Verses to look at: Isaiah 10:1–4; Amos 4:1–3; Matthew 6:19–21)

5) Does James teach that it is a sin to be wealthy? Does the Bible teach this? How would you support your answer?

_____

_____

_____

_____

_____

_____

_____

_____

_____

(Verses to look at: Deuteronomy 8:18; Proverbs 10:22; 1 Timothy 6:10, 17)

6) Does James imply that true believers will escape unpleasantness and difficulty in this life?

_____

_____

_____

_____

_____

_____

_____

_____

_____

_____

(Verses to look at: John 16:33; Acts 14:22; Romans 8:18; 2 Timothy 3:12)

7) How does James counsel his readers to respond in times of trouble? Why?

_____

_____

_____

_____

_____

_____

_____

_____

_____

(Verses to look at: 2 Corinthians 4:17; 1 Peter 1: 6–7; 2:21–23; 4:7)

8) What did James teach about Christ's return? In what ways is this a comforting truth?

_____

_____

_____

_____

_____

_____

_____

_____

_____

_____

(Verses to look at: Romans 13:12; Hebrews 10:25; 1 Peter 4:7; 1 John 2:18)

9) Why did James argue that the Jewish custom of swearing oaths was unnecessary and improper in the church?

_____

_____

_____

_____

_____

_____

_____

_____

_____

(Verses to look at: Matthew 5:33–37; Ephesians 4:25; Colossians 3:9)

Cross Reference

Read Job 42.

¹ *Then Job answered the L*ORD *and said:*

² *"I know that You can do everything,*

And that no purpose of Yours can be withheld from You.
3 *You asked, 'Who is this who hides counsel without knowledge?'*
Therefore I have uttered what I did not understand,
Things too wonderful for me, which I did not know.
4 *Listen, please, and let me speak;*
You said, 'I will question you, and you shall answer Me.'
5 *"I have heard of You by the hearing of the ear,*
But now my eye sees You.
6 *Therefore I abhor myself,*
And repent in dust and ashes."
7 *And so it was, after the Lord had spoken these words to Job, that the Lord said to Eliphaz the Temanite, "My wrath is aroused against you and your two friends, for you have not spoken of Me what is right, as My servant Job has.*
8 *"Now therefore, take for yourselves seven bulls and seven rams, go to My servant Job, and offer up for yourselves a burnt offering; and My servant Job shall pray for you. For I will accept him, lest I deal with you according to your folly; because you have not spoken of Me what is right, as My servant Job has."*
9 *So Eliphaz the Temanite and Bildad the Shuhite and Zophar the Naamathite went and did as the Lord commanded them; for the Lord had accepted Job.*
10 *And the Lord restored Job's losses when he prayed for his friends. Indeed the Lord gave Job twice as much as he had before.*
11 *Then all his brothers, all his sisters, and all those who had been his acquaintances before, came to him and ate food with him in his house; and they consoled him and comforted him for all the adversity that the Lord had brought upon him. Each one gave him a piece of silver and each a ring of gold.*
12 *Now the Lord blessed the latter days of Job more than his beginning; for he had fourteen thousand sheep, six thousand camels, one thousand yoke of oxen, and one thousand female donkeys.*
13 *He also had seven sons and three daughters.*
14 *And he called the name of the first Jemimah, the name of the second Keziah, and the name of the third Keren-Happuch.*
15 *In all the land were found no women so beautiful as the daughters of Job; and their father gave them an inheritance among their brothers.*
16 *After this Job lived one hundred and forty years, and saw his children and grandchildren for four generations.*
17 *So Job died, old and full of days.*

Exploring the Meaning

10) Was there a purpose for Job's suffering? What?

_____

_____

_____

_____

_____

_____

_____

(Verses to look at: Romans 5:3–5; 8:28, 29; 2 Corinthians 12:7–10)

11) Read Exodus 34:6–7. Why is it wise to remember God's character in times of difficulty?

_____

_____

_____

_____

_____

_____

_____

_____

(Verses to look at: Numbers 14:18; 1 Chronicles 21:13; 2 Chronicles 30:9; Lamentations 3:22; Joel 2:13; Jonah 4:2; Luke 6:36)

12) Read Philippians 2:14. Why is grumbling/complaining about trials something Christians should avoid?

_____

_____

_____

_____

_____

_____

_____

_____

_____

_____

Summing Up . . .

"Wealth may be a blessing, a gift from God bringing the opportunity to do good. But that can only be true of those who are also 'rich in faith' (James 2:5) and 'rich toward God' (Luke 12:21). If wealth is to be a source of blessing and not condemnation, it must not be uselessly hoarded, unjustly gained, self-indulgently spent, or ruthlessly acquired."—*John MacArthur*

Reflecting on the Text

13) Which do you have to watch out for most in your own life: acquiring riches ruthlessly or unjustly, hoarding money uselessly, or spending wealth self-indulgently? What needs to change immediately in your view of wealth and in your handling of it?

_____

_____

_____

_____

_____

_____

_____

_____

_____

_____

14) Different people respond differently to trials. Some become quiet, philosophical, even resigned. Others become sad, hopeless, and despondent. Still others become angry and bitter—while a few put their hope in God and maintain a tangible joy despite their circumstances. What description best characterizes you in times of difficulty?

_____

_____

_____

_____

_____

_____

_____

_____

15) Do you sometimes try to make your promises more convincing with phrases like: "No, really!" or "Cross my heart!" or "I swear to you/to God!" or "I'm not kidding—trust me! If I don't keep my word then you can ..."? How, if at all, does James 5:12 speak to these kinds of exclamations?

_____

_____

Recording Your Thoughts

For further study, see the following passages:

Psalm 78:38

Isaiah 5:8–10

Matthew 6:24

Galatians 6:9

1 Peter 4:12–13

Psalm 86:5, 15

Amos 8:4–10

Matthew 23:16–22

2 Thessalonians 1:4

Isaiah 3:14–15

Matthew 5:10–12

John 15:20

1 Timothy 4:1

Righteous Praying

Opening Thought

1) Different people respond differently to difficulties and suffering. How do the unbelievers you know typically respond? How do the most mature Christians you know respond? How do you usually respond?

_____

_____

_____

_____

_____

_____

2) When was the last time you confessed your sin to another person and had them pray with or for you regarding that sin? Why do many believers find this difficult—often to the point of not doing it at all?

_____

_____

_____

_____

_____

_____

Background of the Passage

In view of the overall context of his epistle, particularly chapter 5, it is not surprising that James brings up the subject of suffering in 5:13. He calls on those who are suffering the persecution discussed in 5:1–11 to pray, since prayer is the source of spiritual endurance. It would have been surprising, if, in a letter to struggling, persecuted believers, James had neglected to mention prayer. A strong commitment to prayer is a prerequisite to enduring suffering and affliction.

The theme of verses 13–18, then, is prayer, which is mentioned in every one of those verses. James's exhortation to prayer embraces the prayer life of the entire church. Individual believers are called to pray in verse 13, the elders in verses 14–15, and the congregation in verse 16. This section also reflects James's compassionate pastoral care for his suffering flock; his main focus is on the casualties of the spiritual battle—the persecuted, weak, defeated believers.

As the context and the content of this section make clear, the subject is not physical illness or healing. Instead, its concern is with healing spiritual weakness, spiritual weariness, spiritual exhaustion, and spiritual depression through prayer, as well as dealing with the suffering and sin that accompanies it. Specifically, James discusses the relationship of prayer to comfort, restoration, fellowship, and power.

The final two verses form a fitting conclusion to the book of James. They express James' primary objective in writing his epistle: to confront those in the assembly of believers who possessed false, dead faith. Here is one last salvation warning regarding those who identify with the church but are not regenerate. But rather than speaking directly to them, James calls on the genuine Christians in the church to do evangelism. He wants the believers to pursue the "make-believers."

Bible Passage

Read James 5:13–20, noting the key words and definitions to the right of the passage.

James 5:13–20

¹³ *Is anyone among you suffering? Let him pray. Is anyone cheerful? Let him sing psalms.*

¹⁴ *Is anyone among you sick? Let him call for the elders of the church, and let them pray over him, anointing him with oil in the name of the Lord.*

¹⁵ *And the prayer of faith will save the sick, and the Lord will raise him up. And if he has committed sins, he will be forgiven.*

¹⁶ *Confess your trespasses to one another, and pray for one another, that you may be healed. The effective, fervent prayer of a righteous man avails much.*

¹⁷ *Elijah was a man with a nature like ours, and he prayed earnestly that it would not rain; and it did not rain on the land for three years and six months.*

¹⁸ *And he prayed again, and the heaven gave rain, and the earth produced its fruit.*

¹⁹ *Brethren, if anyone among you wanders from the truth, and someone turns him back,*

²⁰ *let him know that he who turns a sinner from the error of his way will save a soul from death and cover a multitude of sins.*

suffering (v. 13)—The antidote to the suffering caused by evil treatment or persecution is seeking God's comfort through prayer.

Let him sing psalms. (v. 13)—The natural response of a joyful heart is to sing praise to God.

sick (vv. 14–15)—James directs those who are "sick," meaning weakened by their suffering, to call for the elders of the church for strength, support, and prayer.

anointing him with oil (v. 14)—literally "rubbing him with oil": (1) possibly this is a reference to ceremonial anointing; (2) on the other hand, James may have had in mind medical treatment of believers physically bruised and battered by persecution. Perhaps it is better to understand the anointing in a metaphorical sense of the elders' encouraging, comforting, and strengthening the believer.

prayer of faith (v. 15)—the prayer offered on their behalf by the elders

save the sick (v. 15)—deliver them from their suffering because they have been weakened by their infirmity, not from their sin, which was confessed

committed sins ... be forgiven (v. 15)—not by the elders, since God alone can forgive sins; that those who are suffering called for the elders implies they had a contrite, repentant heart, and that part of their time with the overseers would involve confessing their sins to God

Confess your trespasses (v. 16)—Mutual honesty, openness, and sharing of needs will enable believers to uphold each other in the spiritual struggle.

The effective ... avails much (v. 16)—The energetic, passionate prayers of godly men have the power to accomplish much.

Elijah ... prayed ... he prayed again (vv. 17–18)—Elijah provides one of the most notable illustrations of the power of prayer in the Old Testament. His prayers (not mentioned in the Old Testament account) both initiated and ended a three and a half year drought.

if anyone among you (v. 19)—This introduces a third category of people in the church (see vv. 13–14)—those professing believers who have strayed from the truth.

wanders from the truth (v. 19)—apostatizes from the faith he or she once professed. Such people are in grave danger (v. 20), and the church must call them back to the true faith.

sinner (v. 20)—a word used to describe the unregenerate (see James 4:8); James has in mind here those with dead faith (see 2:14–26), not sinning, true believers

the error of his way (v. 20)—Those who go astray doctrinally (v. 19) will also manifest an errant lifestyle, one not lived according to biblical principles.

save a soul from death (v. 20)—A person who wanders from the truth puts his soul in jeopardy. The "death" in view is not physical death, but eternal death—eternal separation from God and eternal punishment in hell. Knowing how high the stakes are should motivate Christians to aggressively pursue such people.

cover a multitude of sins (v. 20)—Since even one sin is enough to condemn a person to hell, James's use of the word "multitude" emphasizes the hopeless condition of lost, unregenerate sinners. The good news of the gospel is that God's forgiving grace (which is greater than any sin; Rom. 5:20) is available to those who turn from their sins and exercise faith in the Lord Jesus Christ (Eph. 2:8–9).

Understanding the Text

3) What kind of suffering does James refer to in v. 13? Is the context speaking of physical sickness or spiritual weakness?

_____

_____

_____

_____

4) How can prayer make a difference—really—in the life of a struggling saint?

_____

_____

_____

_____

_____

_____

(Verses to look at: Psalm 27:13–14; Jonah 2:7; Philippians 4:6–7; 1 Peter 5:7)

5) Why was Elijah mentioned as a stellar example of faithful praying?

_____

_____

_____

_____

_____

(Verses to look at: 1 Kings 17:1–7; 18:1–2; 41–46)

6) What does it mean to "wander from the truth"?

_____

_____

_____

_____

_____

_____

(Verses to look at: Hebrews 5:12–6:9; 1 John 2:19)

7) To what group does James give the label "sinner" in v. 20?

_____

_____

_____

_____

_____

_____

_____

_____

Cross-Reference

Read Matthew 13:24–43.

²⁴ *Another parable He put forth to them, saying: "The kingdom of heaven is like a man who sowed good seed in his field;*

²⁵ *"but while men slept, his enemy came and sowed tares among the wheat and went his way.*

²⁶ *"But when the grain had sprouted and produced a crop, then the tares also appeared.*

²⁷ *"So the servants of the owner came and said to him, 'Sir, did you not sow good seed in your field? How then does it have tares?'*

²⁸ *"He said to them, 'An enemy has done this.' The servants said to him, 'Do you want us then to go and gather them up?'*

²⁹ *"But he said, 'No, lest while you gather up the tares you also uproot the wheat with them.*

³⁰ *'Let both grow together until the harvest, and at the time of harvest I will say to the reapers, "First gather together the tares and bind them in bundles to burn them, but gather the wheat into my barn." ' "*

³¹ *Another parable He put forth to them, saying: "The kingdom of heaven is like a mustard seed, which a man took and sowed in his field,*

³² *"which indeed is the least of all the seeds; but when it is grown it is greater than the herbs and becomes a tree, so that the birds of the air come and nest in its branches."*

³³ *Another parable He spoke to them: "The kingdom of heaven is like leaven, which a woman took and hid in three measures of meal till it was all leavened."*

³⁴ *All these things Jesus spoke to the multitude in parables; and without a parable He did not speak to them,*

³⁵ *that it might be fulfilled which was spoken by the prophet, saying:*
"I will open My mouth in parables;
I will utter things kept secret from the foundation of the world."

36 *Then Jesus sent the multitude away and went into the house. And His disciples came to Him, saying, "Explain to us the parable of the tares of the field."*

37 *He answered and said to them: "He who sows the good seed is the Son of Man.*

38 *"The field is the world, the good seeds are the sons of the kingdom, but the tares are the sons of the wicked one.*

39 *"The enemy who sowed them is the devil, the harvest is the end of the age, and the reapers are the angels.*

40 *"Therefore as the tares are gathered and burned in the fire, so it will be at the end of this age.*

41 *"The Son of Man will send out His angels, and they will gather out of His kingdom all things that offend, and those who practice lawlessness,*

42 *"and will cast them into the furnace of fire. There will be wailing and gnashing of teeth.*

43 *"Then the righteous will shine forth as the sun in the kingdom of their Father. He who has ears to hear, let him hear!"*

Exploring the Meaning

8) What does this passage add to your understanding of James's teaching of the danger of wandering from the truth?

_____

_____

_____

_____

_____

_____

(Verses to look at: see Isaiah 66:24; Daniel 12:2; Matthew 13:40, 42, 50; Mark 9:43–49; Romans 6:23; 2 Thessalonians 1:8–9; Revelation 20:11–15)

9) Read Acts 3:19. What does this teach about the necessity of sinners turning from sin? Salvation requires what?

_____

_____

_____

_____

_____

_____

(Verses to look at: Matthew 18:3; Luke 1:16–17; Acts 9:35; 2 Corinthians 3:16; 1 Peter 2:25)

Summing Up . . .

"Maintaining open, sharing, and praying relationships with other Christians will help keep believers from bottoming out in their spiritual lives. Such relationships help give the spiritual strength that provides victory over sin. And they also provide godly pressure to confess and forsake sins before they become overwhelming to the point of total spiritual defeat....

"God has granted to all believers the ministry of reconciling wandering souls to Himself. When the evidence indicates a professed believer's faith is not real, true Christians, knowing the terrible threat of eternal death that person faces, must make it their goal to turn him back from his sin to genuine saving faith in God."—*John MacArthur*

Reflecting on the Text

10) Is it your habit to pray regularly for Christians who are discouraged and struggling? If not, why not?

_____

_____

_____

_____

_____

_____

11) How is such a practice dependent largely on deep involvement in a body of believers?

_____

_____

_____

_____

_____

_____

12) Are you spiritually defeated, discouraged, and/or depressed right now? Make a list of believers (don't forget your church leaders!) from whom you could solicit prayer support. Before another day passes, contact these folks and share your situation and need with them.

_____

_____

_____

_____

_____

_____

13) Can you think of some professing believers in your church who, according to the tests of true faith found here in James, may not be actually saved? Pray for them right now. Ask God also to show you if (and when?) you should lovingly express your concerns. If you feel uneasy about this (and just to be wise, even if you don't!), talk your plan over first with a mature Christian you deeply respect.

_____

_____

_____

_____

Recording Your Thoughts

_____

_____

_____

_____

_____

_____

_____

_____

_____

_____

_____

_____

_____

_____

_____

_____

For further study, see the following passages:

Leviticus 14:18	Numbers 11:2	Psalm 5:10
Psalm 55:22	Proverbs 13:6, 22	Isaiah 43:25
Daniel 9:9	Matthew 25:41, 46	Mark 2:7
Mark 6:13	Luke 15:7, 10	Acts 14:15
Acts 26:18, 20	James 4:8	Revelation 21:8

The MacArthur Bible Collection

John MacArthur, General Editor

The MacArthur Study Bible

From the moment you pick it up, you'll know it's a classic. Featuring the word-for-word accuracy of the New King James Version, *The MacArthur Study Bible* is perfect for serious study. Pastor/teacher John MacArthur has compiled more than 20,000 study notes, a 200-page topical index and numerous charts, maps, outlines, and articles to create *The MacArthur Study Bible*. This Bible has been crafted with the finest materials in a variety of handsome bindings, including hardcover and indexed bonded leather. Winner of "The 1998 Study Bible of the Year Award."

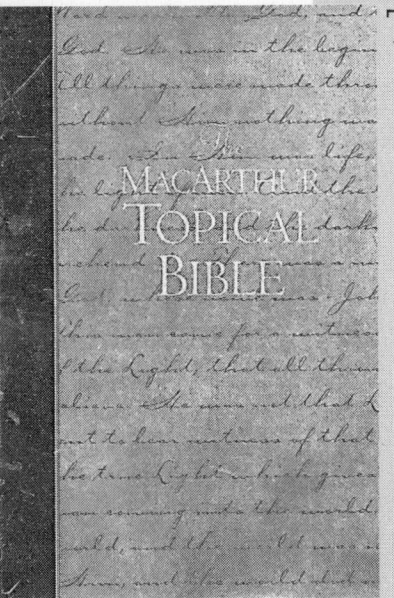

The MacArthur Topical Bible

In the excellent tradition of *Nave's Topical Bible,* this newly created reference book incorporates thousands of topics and ideas, both traditional and contemporary, for believers today and in the new millennium. Carefully researched and prepared by Dr. John MacArthur and the faculty of Masters Seminary, *The MacArthur Topical Bible* will quickly become the reference of choice of all serious Bible students. Using the New King James translation, this Bible is arranged alphabetically by topic and is completely cross-referenced. This exhaustive resource is an indispensible tool for the topical study of God's Word.

The MacArthur Bible Studies

These first ten study guides in a 16-volume set from noted Bible scholar John MacArthur take readers on a journey through biblical texts to discover what lies beneath the surface, focusing on meaning and context, and then reflecting on the explored passage or concept. With probing questions that guide the reader toward application, as well as ample space for journaling, *The MacArthur Bible Studies* are an invaluable tool for Bible students of all ages.

- Ephesians
- Mark
- 1 Samuel
- Romans
- Ruth & Esther
- Daniel
- John
- Acts
- Galatians
- 1 & 2 Peter
- James
- Nehemiah
- Revelation
- Hebrews
- 1 Corinthians
- 1 & 2 Timothy

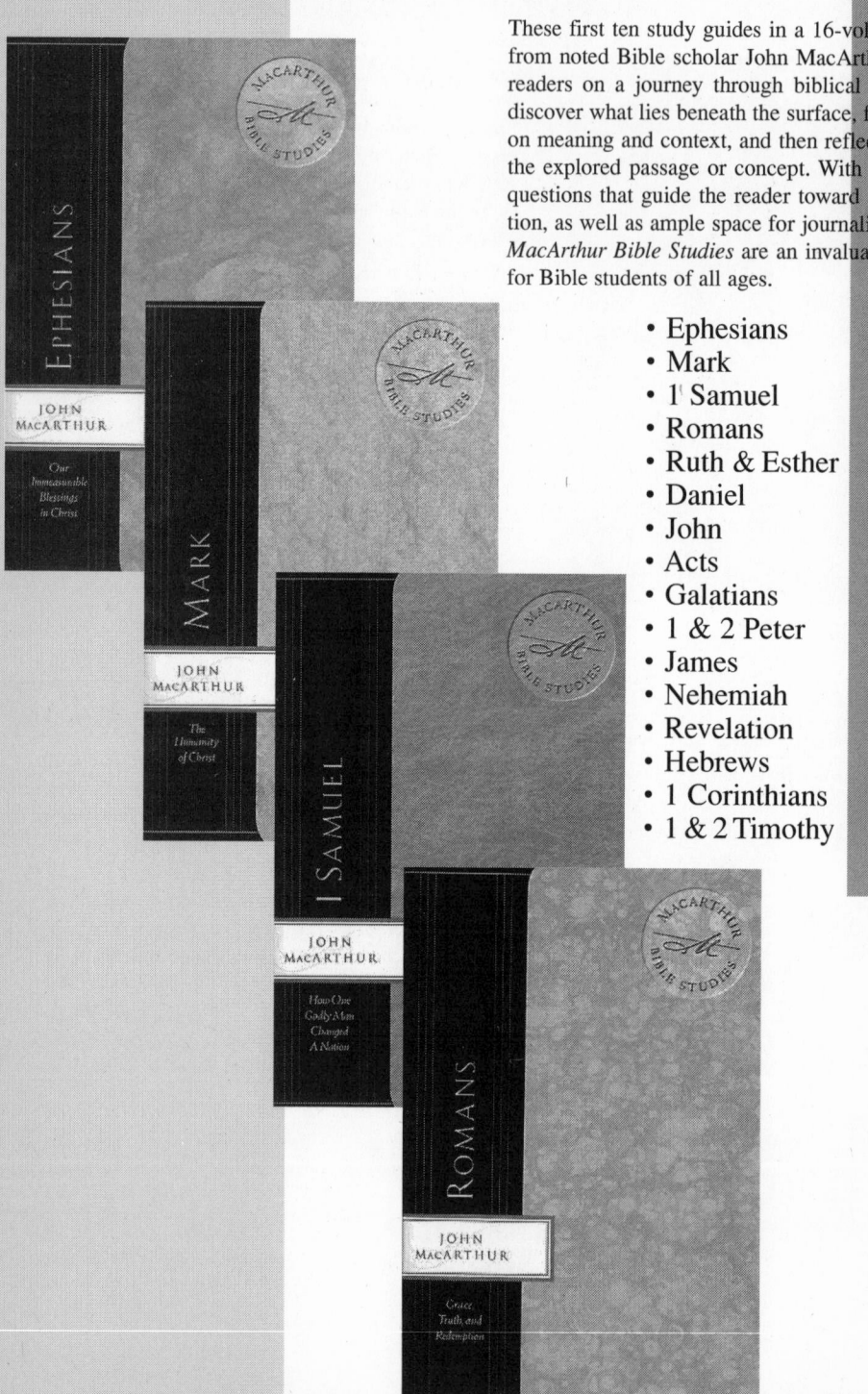